DAVID RUNCIMAN

PROFILE BOOKS

First published in Great Britain in 2014 by
PROFILE BOOKS LTD
3A Exmouth House
Pine Street
London EC1R 0JH
www.profilebooks.com

COGNI+IVE

3 5 7 9 10 8 6 4 2

Designed by Jade Design
www.jadedesign.co.uk

Printed and bound in Italy by L.E.G.O. SpA–Lavis (TN)

A CIP catalogue record for this book is available from the British Library.

ISBN 978 1 78125 257 4
eISBN 978 1 78283 056 6
Enhanced eBook ISBN 978 1 78283 135 8

POLITICS

CONTENTS

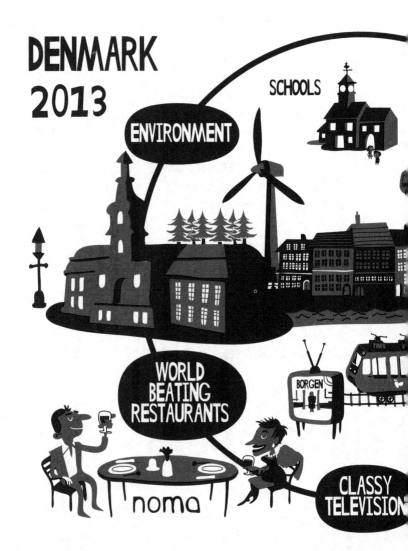

DENMARK
2013

ENVIRONMENT

SCHOOLS

WORLD
BEATING
RESTAURANTS

noma

BORGEN

CLASSY
TELEVISION

INTRODUCTION
POLITICS

SOCIAL SECURITY

HOSPITALS

TRANSPORT SYSTEM

Politics matters.

If you live in Syria today, you are stuck in a kind of hell: life is frightening, violent, unpredictable, impoverished and, for all too many Syrians, short. As I write, estimates for the number of Syrians killed in the civil war range from 80,000 to 200,000. (The gulf between the estimates is a sign of how bad things are: the dead have disappeared into a cloud of disinformation.) The people who have seen their quality of life displaced runs into the millions. The number who have seen their quality of life depleted because of the violence includes just about everybody in the country (unemployment in 2014 is reckoned to be about 60 per cent). No one in their right mind would choose to live in Syria right now.

If you are lucky enough to live in Denmark, you are in what is by any historical standards a version of heaven: life is comfortable, prosperous,

SYRIA 2014

IS RESPONSIBLE FOR EVERYTHING BAD
SYRIANS KILLED
8
WE DIDN'T INVENT THE RELIGIOUS & ETHNIC DIVISIONS

protected and civilised, and it lasts. The world envies Denmark its fantastic restaurants, its classy television programmes, its elegant design culture, its generous social security provisions, its environmentally friendly lifestyles. Denmark comes at or near the top of international comparisons that measure quality of life and the contentment of citizens. Danes regularly report that they are happier than anyone else. Perhaps not everyone would choose to live in Denmark: the downside, like many versions of heaven, is that it might be a little boring. But if you had no prior attachments, you'd pick Denmark over Syria any day.

The difference isn't that Danes are better people than Syrians. They aren't inherently nicer or smarter: people are pretty much people the world over. Nor have Danes been blessed with greater natural advantages. If anything, it's the reverse: Syria is part of the fertile crescent that was once the birthplace of human civilisation; Denmark is a bleak northern outpost with few natural resources

MILLIONS OF
SYRIANS
DISPLACED

3

of its own. Denmark is full of nice things, but not many of them grow out of the ground. (The restaurants that have made Denmark's gastronomic reputation specialise in local produce, but they transform it with the aid of modern technology; no one would pay those prices for what the Danish soil produces on its own.)

The difference between Denmark and Syria is politics. Politics has helped make Denmark what it is. And politics has helped make Syria what it is.

To say that politics makes the difference is not to say that politics is responsible for everything good that happens in one place and everything bad that happens somewhere else. Danes aren't happy because their politics make them happy: politicians seem to annoy and aggrieve the Danes just as much as they do people everywhere. Danish politicians can take some of the credit for their social security or transport systems, but they can hardly claim to be the ones who made the restaurants world-beaters or the design so desirable. Likewise, Syria's current politicians are to blame for plenty of the misery stalking their country (as are politicians from Moscow to Riyadh who have been stoking it), but they didn't invent the religious and ethnic divisions that are behind so much of the violence. The civil war has pitted Sunni against Shia; it is being fuelled by deep differences of culture and history; it was triggered by the chance effects of recession and drought. Politics doesn't create all human passions or hatreds. Nor is politics responsible for every natural disaster or economic set-back that takes place. But it either amplifies them or it moderates them. That's the difference it makes.

Denmark today looks like a country that enjoys political

stability because its people have nothing serious to fight about. Danes might be antsy about immigration, like many Europeans. But, compared with Syria, there exist none of the ethnic or cultural fissures that would provoke a civil war. As well as being peaceful and prosperous, Denmark is also a broadly secular society: religion doesn't overshadow public life, even though it does occasionally intrude. But Denmark wasn't always like this. Five hundred years ago it was more like Syria: a fragile, tempestuous, hard-scrabble place, shot through with religious conflict and violent disagreements. During the sixteenth and seventeenth centuries, when Denmark, like the rest of Europe, was regularly tearing itself apart, you would have been hard pressed to know whether it was better to live there or in Syria. Life was cheap everywhere. If anything, Denmark was the really dangerous place to be, because of the endless spill-over of conflict with its Scandinavian neighbours. For most of its history Denmark stood at the crossroads for war in Europe. Syria's borders today are an arbitrary construct, imposed on the country by victorious rival powers. But so too are Denmark's.

Yet, despite this, Denmark has made the transition from war to peace, and from a subsistence economy to a wealthy one. It did so by arriving at the social and political institutions that enabled its people to co-exist peacefully with each other and with their neighbours. How this happened is not easy to explain. The puzzle is that good politics is both a symptom and a cause of the transition. Politics works in Denmark because it has made Danes more tolerant. But it also works because Danes have learned a tolerance for politics. These are the two sides to any successful political arrangement. There is the politics that is produced by stable institutions: all the arguments and disagreements that somehow stop short of war. And there is the politics that produces stable institutions: all the arguments and agreements that somehow bring war to a stop. Politics cannot be reduced to any particular set of institutions. It precedes them, and it emerges from them.

What these two sides of political life have in common is that they both combine choice with constraint. Politics is about the collective choices that bind groups of people to live in a particular way. It is also about the collective binds that give people a real choice in how they live. Without real choice there is no politics. If it were the case that successful political institutions were the automatic product of particular historical circumstances – give me the right climate, culture, economy, religion, demographics, and I'll give you democracy – then life would be a lot simpler. But it's not that simple. Political institutions are still shaped by human choices, and human beings always retain the capacity to screw them up. Equally, if it were the case that the right political institutions did away with the need for choice – give me democracy, and I'll give you peace, prosperity, fancy restaurants, a quiet life – then life would also be simpler and a lot duller. But even in Denmark the successful functioning of political institutions depends on the choices people make: choices made by politicians and by voters, choices about what laws to have and about whether to obey them. Some of these choices can be agonising: even in rich, happy countries some political decisions are matters of life and death. Nothing is automatic in politics. Everything depends on the contingent interplay between choice and constraint: constraint under conditions of choice; choice under conditions of constraint.

So we can say that the difference between Syria and Denmark is simple: it's politics. We can also say that the reason for the difference between Syria and Denmark is complex: it's politics. In this short book I want to try to bridge the gap between the simplicity and the complexity by answering three big questions. First, how can the same word – *politics* – encompass such different societies as safe, boring Denmark and chaotic, miserable Syria? What do heaven and hell have in common? It is tempting to think that one represents the absence of politics (heaven) and the other represents the failure of politics (hell). But in fact they reveal the different sides of politics. In the first chapter I aim to show what they have in common. The point of connection is the control of violence, which is the defining characteristic of every political society. Thinking about violence is a starting-point for considering where politics comes from, what makes it different from other activities and why it still makes all the difference.

Second, how can politics continue to make all the difference when we are living through a time of such rapid technological change? Denmark is a tiny player in the globalised economy. But even the big players – China, the United States – often seem at the mercy of forces far more powerful than they are: the market, the internet, the environment. So many things appear beyond the power of politicians to control. What role is left for politicians in the face of a globalised technological revolution? In the second chapter I explore the relationship between politics and technology, looking at how they impact on each other. Technology often appears to be in the lead, with politics playing catch-up. Technology is very difficult to control. But it is still true that the only people who can control it are politicians.

Third, if politics is what makes the difference, why do we tolerate such vast discrepancies between the world's most successful states and its least successful ones? Why don't we export what works to the places where nothing seems to work? Why don't we try harder to make Syria more like Denmark? There are practical difficulties, of course. But this isn't just a question of practicality. There is also a basic question of justice. Human beings aren't so different, in what they hope for, in what they can achieve and in what they need to help get them there. Yet the global gap between the richest and poorest is as big as it has ever been. Why can't politics do more to rescue the nearly 2 billion people

who still have to live (and die) on less than $2 a day? In the third chapter I look at the moral question we need to ask of our politics and of ourselves: why do we tolerate so much injustice? Politics is not the same as morality, but morality impinges on politics as much as it does on anything else we do. In the end, morality exposes the limits of politics. We can't have justice without politics. But politics still fails the demands of justice on the largest scale.

The first chapter explains what politics is (at its best and at its worst). The second chapter explains why it still matters (even in the age of Google). The third chapter explains what its limits are (in the face of massive global inequality). Then, in the epilogue, I explore the risks that lie ahead. The world remains an intensely dangerous place, though in many places much less dangerous than it used to be. Some of the dangers we face are unprecedented. Is it realistic to think that politics will save us after all?

1
VIOLENCE

CONSENSUS AND COERCION

The control of violence lies at the heart of politics. This doesn't mean that all politics is inherently violent. Lots of forms of politics have no violence in them at all: argument, discussion, agreement are often peaceful activities undertaken by people who wouldn't dream of attacking each other physically. Sometimes fights do break out in parliaments, which is both hilarious and shocking. But it's not meant to happen like that, and in all parliaments there are plenty of rules in place to try to ensure that it doesn't happen. (In the British parliament you are not even allowed to accuse your opponents of lying, in case it provokes them.) Nor is it true that all violence is inherently political. If you get mugged, you don't enter into a political relationship with your mugger (though a mugging could have political consequences if it made you angry enough to try to push for a change in the law). The key to politics is not the violence as such. It is the control.

There are two ways to think about politics as controlling violence. One is that violence can be used as a tool of control to draw people into ongoing relationships of authority and

11

obedience. This is control *through* violence. If I know that you have the consistent power to hurt me, I will adjust my behaviour accordingly, to the point where you may not need to threaten me in order to get me to do what you want. I'll do what you want anyway, because of my knowledge of the power you have. The prospect of violence can shape people's behaviour without anyone getting hurt. All politics contains an element of this sort of pressure: we behave law-abidingly because of the implicit threat of what would happen to us if we didn't. But the other side of politics is the control *of* violence. Politics enables people to reach agreements about how to deal with violence, about who should have access to it and the circumstances in which it should be used. All political systems contain agreements of this sort as well: the people who control us through violence are the beneficiaries of our shared understanding about how to control the use of violence. We behave law-abidingly because we accept that lawmakers and law-enforcers have the right to tell us what to do. Without that shared understanding there would be no politics. There would just be an endless series of muggings.

In the introduction I said that politics is about choice under conditions of constraint and constraint under conditions of choice. But we can be more specific than this. Lots of human activities fit that description: marriage, for instance. You can choose whom you want to marry, but if the other person doesn't want to marry you, too bad: there's the constraint. Likewise, once you have found a willing partner, getting married imposes shared burdens on both of you, backed up by the force of law. It is possible to argue, and many feminists do argue, that any marriage is basically political. That is certainly the case if one partner uses the threat of violence to condition the behaviour of the other. Abusive marriages are crude and very unpleasant forms of power politics. But not all marriages are like this. Human beings are capable of relating to each other through love, even when their choices are constrained. It would be a big mistake to think that all human relationships can be reduced to politics.

What's specific to politics is the relationship over time between consensus and coercion. Politics presupposes a collective agreement about the use of force. Because there is agreement, force is not always necessary. Because there is force, agreement is not always sufficient. Politics needs both. This is what connects Denmark and Syria. Denmark looks like a highly consensual society. But even Denmark has an army, a police force and a prison system. Even in Denmark the state has the power to compel its citizens to behave in ways they don't like: it can make them pay tax, or force them to face the consequences. Syria, by contrast, looks like a highly coercive society. But even in Syria people must agree on the use of force for political institutions to function at all. There is currently no consensus between the various sides in the civil war, yet there must be some consensus on the different sides for the war to continue. Assad loyalists recognise the legitimacy of the regime and accept its right to defend itself. Their opponents reject that right while accepting the right of the opposition to use force against it. If Syria were nothing but a coercive society, there would be no civil war. There would just be anarchy, which is no politics at all. The fight is a political one between competing views about who is entitled to use force against others.

Denmark and Syria both exist on a spectrum in which consensus and coercion are combined. This is the single spectrum of politics. But they are at opposite ends of the spectrum. In Denmark consensus limits coercion: there is enough agreement that the use of force can be kept to a relative minimum. In Syria coercion limits consensus: there is enough violence for the scope for agreement to remain minimal. One spectrum, two ends: that's what makes it possible to compare these two societies and also fundamentally to distinguish them.

There is a more cynical view. Christian Jungersen's novel *The Exception* (2006) is set in a Danish humanitarian organisation whose employees are tasked with investigating war crimes in the former Yugoslavia. What could be more different than a comfortable office in Copenhagen and a Bosnian death camp? The Danes in the story are women with safe, comfortable lives; the criminals they are trying to track are displaced and deeply dangerous men. But Jungersen shows the two worlds mirroring each other. The women in the office bully, threaten and persecute each other; small acts of aggression – a slammed door, a hostile glance – escalate into life-threatening violence. In this telling, consensual societies are simply hiding the horribly coercive impulses that stain all human relationships. Nice Denmark is as nasty underneath as anywhere else. If anything, the niceness makes the nastiness harder to control because the aggressors are in denial about what they are doing. Do-gooding politics can be a façade that enables the horrible things it is meant to prevent.

Cynicism always has a place in politics. But this is too cynical. It's true that any form of consensus has the capacity to hide violence instead of limiting it. The BBC, one of the most respectable and do-gooding institutions in British public life, turned out to be an excellent place for paedophiles to operate because no one was looking for them. It's also true that societies in which violence is visible everywhere – such as present-day Syria – can conceal the myriad acts of kindness that take place within private life and between personal friends. Bad things happen in nice places, and nice things happen in bad places. But that doesn't mean the places themselves are hard to tell apart. There is still a fundamental difference between Denmark and Syria. Societies in which violence is under an agreed system of political control are better places to live in than those in which it is not.

Political consensus doesn't abolish violence: pockets of horror exist everywhere. In some circumstances political consensus encourages violence, especially on the part of the people charged with controlling it. Policemen can still do the most terrible things. These are the dark themes of Scandinavian crime fiction and one reason it's so popular all over the world. But the backdrop for Scandinavian crime fiction is societies in which violence has not been allowed to run out of control, unlike in Syria. That's the difference.

THE INVENTION OF THE STATE

The philosopher who did most to put the control of violence at the heart of thinking about politics was a seventeenth-century Englishman called Thomas Hobbes. In doing so, he explained what lies at the basis of modern political life and what makes it different from what went before. Violence was out of control in Hobbes's world. He produced three versions of his political philosophy in little more than a decade: one in 1640 (*The Elements of Law*), just before the start of the English civil war; one in 1642 (*De Cive*), republished in 1647 while the fighting was going on; and one in 1651 (*Leviathan*), when it was effectively over. The last of these is the book for which he is known today. *Leviathan* is his masterpiece. It is perhaps the greatest work of political philosophy in the English language.

During most of this period Hobbes was living in Paris, having fled England to escape the violence. Thanks to his eagerness to get out of harm's way, his life eventually spanned the best part of a century: he was born in 1588, the year of the Spanish Armada, and died in 1679, as English politics was gearing itself up for its next revolution (the 'Glorious Revolution' of 1688 that initiated the age of parliamentary government). It was a tempestuous and frightening time to be alive. England was bad. Much of Europe was worse. The Thirty Years War, which consumed the continent from 1618 to 1648, was a true bloodbath: a maelstrom of religious, ethnic and dynastic conflict that swallowed up entire communities (that's one reason why you would not want to have found yourself in Denmark at the wrong moment in its history). The viciousness of the current fighting in Syria is sometimes seen as a reflection of the peculiarly violence-prone mindset of the Islamic world. This is not true. Even Syria pales in comparison with what happened in early to mid-seventeenth-century Christian Europe, where the technology of mass destruction was nowhere near as advanced as it is today. Without the help of chemical weapons or precision bombs, Christians still slaughtered each other in their millions.

Though he wrote it three times in three different sets of circumstances – once when England still had a king, once when there was no agreed government, once when parliament was in charge – Hobbes's basic political philosophy never changed. Civil war was a disaster, and the first task in thinking about politics was how to avoid it. To this end, Hobbes conducted a thought experiment. Imagine a world without politics. Human beings, Hobbes thought, are naturally competitive: they want to seem better, stronger, more powerful than each other. They are also naturally vulnerable: even the strongest individuals can be taken down by the weakest when their backs are turned. As a result, the natural condition of mankind is a state of war. Competitive, vulnerable human beings will end up trying to kill each other.

This is not because most people are naturally vicious or because they enjoy violence (though a few may). It's because they can't trust each other: they are naturally suspicious. 'And from this diffidence of one another', Hobbes wrote, 'there is no way for any man to secure himself, so reasonable as anticipation; that is, by force or wiles, to master the persons of all men he can.' Even if you know that you are better off living in peace, and even if you know that every one else knows this, you can't be sure that other people won't see you as a threat. And anyone who might see you as a threat therefore poses a threat, because of what can happen when your back is turned. So you'd better take them out first. A world without politics is one in which violence is bound to run out of control: an endless series of muggings.

It is often assumed that Hobbes's 'state of nature' – where, as he notoriously put it, life is 'solitary, poor, nasty, brutish and short' – corresponds to a condition of civil war. It doesn't. There is a big difference for Hobbes between a world without politics and a world where politics has gone wrong. The English civil war was a result of a terrible fall-ing-out about politics among people who couldn't agree what politics should be. Is it rule by kings or by parliaments? Does it require religious freedom or conformity? Is it meant to protect privilege or to correct it? Hobbes's answer to all these questions was that they were beside the point. Politics is meant to preserve the peace.

The English civil war, like the Syrian civil war, was not a state of anarchy. It was a fight between highly politicised groups that possessed the power to keep the conflict going (one meagre consolation of the state of nature is that mis-trust between individuals would make it hard to sustain war on this scale). The purpose of Hobbes's thought experiment was to transcend the world of politics gone wrong. He was looking for something that even the different sides in the civil war could agree on. They couldn't agree on what sort of politics they wanted. So Hobbes gave them a different choice: politics or non-politics. Faced with that choice, anyone in their right mind would choose politics.

What did it mean to choose politics? For Hobbes it meant agreeing that the only possible solution to the problem of violence in the state of nature was to put the power to control violence in the hands of a single decision-maker. Hobbes called this decision-maker the 'sovereign'. (It didn't have to be a single individual, just something capable of speaking with a single voice, whether a king *or* a parliament.) We all want peace, but we won't achieve peace among ourselves because we can never agree on who poses the most serious threat to our safety. The job of the sovereign is to take that decision for us: effectively to decide who or what poses a threat to peace. If we all agree to that, the sovereign will have the power to keep the peace, because no one will have the power to challenge the sovereign's decision. Sovereignty is therefore a kind of monopoly. It is not strictly a monopoly on violence, since there will always be pockets of domestic and criminal violence, even in the most peaceful societies. Instead, sovereignty is a monopoly on the right to use coercive force as a solution to human conflict. It is the power to make law and to enforce it. Only sovereigns are allowed to hurt people without any comeback.

Present-day readers often find Hobbes shocking. 'Hobbesian' has become a by-word for the bleakest possible view of human nature: one that imagines we are all trigger-happy paranoiacs who need strong government to stop us from killing each other. This is totally unfair. Hobbes was essentially an optimist who thought that people were killing each other only because they had failed to ask the basic question about politics: what is it for? If they could focus on that, the reasons for fighting would fall away. In fact, Hobbes seemed to think that a political society in which everyone accepted the right of a sovereign power to take the life-and-death decisions would be happy and free. The miserable depiction of the state of nature for which he remains famous is only one half of the story. It's designed to point out how different life with a stable government could be: for 'solitary, poor, nasty, brutish and short' read 'convivial, rich, nice, civilised and long'. In other words, think Denmark. If you showed Hobbes contemporary Denmark, I don't think he would feel confounded by all the niceness. He would more likely feel vindicated. 'I told you so', he might say: take the religious feuding and the fearful insecurity out of politics and you can get to paradise, or at least the closest thing to paradise this world has to offer.

Of course, Hobbes would still recognise the cruelty and paranoia described in *The Exception*: given how human beings are, a murderous free-for-all is still possible any-where, even in a Copenhagen office. But he'd think it a big mistake to assume that the state of nature is the default con-dition of all human relationships or that civilisation is just a veneer to conceal the nastiness. Stable politics gives human beings the chance to escape from violence. If some refuse to take that chance, more fool them. Most of us will use the opportunity to create a new set of relationships based on trust and mutual benefit. Hobbes called this civil existence 'artificial', because it was man-made, not natural. But artifi-cial in this context doesn't mean fake. It means solid, reli-able, durable (like a well-made car). It means real.

Much more genuinely shocking for us is not what Hobbes's argument says about Denmark but what it implies about Syria. The point of Hobbes's thought experiment was to get his readers to accept that any form of political rule is better than the alternative: chaos. Given a choice of political systems, Hobbes's own preference was for monarchy because he felt there should be no confusion about who the real decision-maker was (parliaments, in his view, were far too prone to in-fighting). But Hobbes's real message was that there is *no* choice: you have to stick with what you've got. When England still had a king, in 1642 – Charles I – Hobbes insisted that nothing should be done to undermine his authority, however unhappy his subjects might be about how he was using it. Don't like his religion? Don't like the taxes he makes you pay? Don't like the wars he's fighting? Tough. But in 1651, when Charles was dead and parliament was in charge, Hobbes instructed his readers to obey their new rulers. Same philosophy, different outcome. Hobbes thought the rebellion against the king had been a desperate, stupid, treacherous act; but once it had succeeded in getting rid of him, he thought it desperate and stupid to prolong the misery. You always obey the people in charge. You never look for alternatives.

So, on this account, all Syrians ought to have stuck with the deeply unpleasant, oppressive and corrupt Assad regime rather than precipitate a civil war. It was wrong to complain about the injustice of living under Assad because, for Hobbes, political justice is only ever what the sovereign says it is. You must obey your rulers until they can no longer keep the peace (only then do you get to choose who has

21

the best chance of protecting you, though once any fighting is over you must go with whoever has won, regardless of how you feel about it). You must never do anything to threaten the peace yourself. To modern-day readers (and to plenty of Hobbes's contemporaries) it sounds like a counsel of despair. It means always putting up with bad government for fear of no government at all. But can't bad government be even worse than no government, especially when it lasts a long time? (And it can last a long time, certainly longer than a single human lifespan: just look at North Korea.) Hobbes's risk-averse approach to politics appears to make it impossible for politically oppressed people to do anything to make their politics better.

In this we are bound to have a different perspective from Hobbes. But that's not because Hobbes was entirely wrong. It's for some of the reasons that Hobbes was right. When he was writing, he wasn't interested in comparing different types of government because he felt no one had yet got a grip on the fundamentals: his aim was to lay the foundations for a new approach that might lead to lasting peace and prosperity. He didn't want his readers thinking that the apparent political choices in front of them were the real ones. He wanted them to think outside the box of seventeenth-century politics. Now we are outside that box. We have Denmark.

In Hobbes's world there was no equivalent to the choice between Denmark and Syria. The available choice was, as he said in *Leviathan*,

THE DIFFERENCE THAT MATTERS IS BETWEEN LUCCA THEN AND DENMARK NOW

between Lucca and Constantinople. Where would you rather find yourself in the seventeenth century: a free Italian city-state (where they wrote 'LIBERTAS' on the walls of the city and allowed citizens to participate in government) or a Turkish sultanate (where all power was concentrated at the top and you could lose you head on the whim of the sultan)? Lucca sounds a lot better. But Hobbes thought it was an empty choice. 'Whether a Commonwealth be monarchical or popular', he wrote, 'the freedom is still the same.' In his view, writing 'LIBERTAS' on your city was never more than window-dressing: government is still government. It didn't much matter where you were in the seventeenth century. We can now see he had a point, though perhaps not quite in the way he meant. The difference that matters is between Lucca then and Denmark now. Compared with the paradise

SCIENCE   COMMERCE   INDUSTRY   RELIGION

DYNAMIC FORCES OF

that is Denmark today, living anywhere three and a half centuries ago was pretty grim: poor, violent, confrontational, unpredictable and unstable.

Truly stable politics is transformative, as Hobbes predicted. Politics doesn't make the difference on its own. But it creates the space in which the dynamic forces of modernity – science, industry, commerce, culture, even religion – can interact to produce very wide-ranging social and material benefits. Once you live in a world where that transformation has been achieved in some places but not in others, your choices are bound to look different: being stuck in Syria could indeed be intolerable. I'll return to this in the third chapter, where I discuss the question of justice within and between different states in the twenty-first century. Wide-ranging social and material benefits may not in the end be

CULTURE

MODERNITY

enough. For now, let me just say that the choice between Denmark and Syria is a long way from the choice between Lucca and Constantinople. Our world is simultaneously an exemplification and a refutation of Hobbes's theory. Past a certain point, Hobbes's argument eats itself.

Yet perhaps what is most alien about Hobbes for a contemporary readership is how minimalist his account of politics seems. Hobbes pares politics down to the absolute basics: power and obedience, coercion and consent. The sovereign makes the laws, and the people obey them. We expect politics to be about much more than this. Where's the room in Hobbes's account for argument and debate, for confrontation and compromise? What's happened to all the posturing and positioning and the endless back-and-forth that we associate with the activity of politics? But in fact Hobbes's minimalism is deceptive. His view of politics lays the foundations for modern political life as we know it. The arguments that we associate with politics – arguments about tax and welfare and rights and responsibilities – are made possible only by a distinctive modern understanding of what it means to exercise political power. Hobbes provides it.

Hobbes understood that you can't have productive political argument without basic political agreement: the back-and-forth depends on an underlying consensus. Sometimes the two sides of politics may still react on each other to produce surprising results: any political argument, however seemingly trivial, always has the capacity to challenge the established political order. A fight about tax rates can lead to a revolution. That's why Hobbes tried to make the relationship between coercion and consent as tight as he could. But what really marks Hobbes out is that he saw that the two go together and that they depend on each other. This approach underpins the idea of the modern state, which is the institution that has come to dominate the political landscape since Hobbes's time. In three crucial respects his thinking marks the transition from the pre-modern to the modern world of politics.

First, Hobbes's political philosophy is self-justifying: it explains politics in terms of the value of politics, not in terms of some external set of values. Ancient and medieval conceptions of politics invariably sought to justify politics with reference to something else. For the ancients, politics rested on an idea of virtue: the point of being a citizen was to lead a virtuous life, to become the best person you could be through politics. For medieval thinkers it rested on religion: earthly power has its source in God's plan for the world (hence, for instance, the doctrine known as the 'Divine Right of Kings'). Hobbes thought this was all rubbish. And worse, it was dangerous rubbish because it just gave human beings one more thing to fight about. Which virtues? Whose God? Civil wars have broken out over far less. He thought politics would only have a secure hold over us if it could prove its usefulness for *us*: people as we are. Politics justified by its utility for regular human beings is a distinctly modern view, and one that still exercises a strong grip.

Second, although Hobbes thought politics is the most important thing, he didn't think it is the all-important thing. The idea that he was a forerunner of totalitarianism is completely wrong. Rather, he was there at the invention of what we have come to call private life: the space in which people are free to do their own thing. The point of settling the basic arguments about politics was to enable people to get on with living their lives unencumbered by endless political disagreement. A stable civic existence gives us the time and the space to do all the other things we want to do, which for Hobbes includes arguing and squabbling and competing and posturing and generally trying to come out on top. These are all potentially fruitful activities if they can only be prevented from becoming deadly. They give rise to invention and romance and excitement and variety and knowledge. They are compatible with both love and grace. They are just not compatible with political monomania.

Hobbes believed it was futile to try to achieve the good life through politics. Instead, politics exists to enable us to pursue the good life for ourselves. He never thought sovereigns could make people happy. He just thought you had no chance of being happy in the absence of a sovereign. This makes Hobbes a 'liberal' in the classic modern European sense: he sees personal fulfilment as requiring political protection but not political instantiation. It is not the only view of modern politics available, but over time it has become the dominant one. Certainly it is the dominant one today.

Finally, Hobbes's idea that politics is founded on an agreement between individuals to let a sovereign take decisions for them was expressed through one of the keywords of modern politics: 'representation'. In *Leviathan* he calls the sovereign 'representative' of his subjects. By this he doesn't mean that the sovereign is answerable to his subjects and certainly not that they can get rid of him if they don't like what he does: that was always anathema for Hobbes. What he means is that the sovereign speaks for his subjects and that they must agree to be spoken for by him. Out of this relationship Hobbes created a political entity that he called a 'state'. A state can't be identified with the sovereign because the sovereign doesn't speak for himself; he speaks for his subjects. Nor can it be identified with his subjects because they don't speak for themselves either: they are spoken for by their sovereign. So a state is what comes into existence when sovereign and subjects are locked together in a relationship of representation. It ceases to exist when that relationship breaks down. Hobbesian politics is both top-down and bottom-up: you need a sovereign at the top making the rules, but you won't have a sovereign able to make the rules if he doesn't speak for the people beneath him.

This is also a distinctly modern idea. Indeed, if you replace the terms 'sovereign' and 'subjects' with 'government' and 'people', you could say it is the modern idea of politics. Modern politics is neither top-down nor bottom-up: it is both at the same time. Pre-modern politics was different. Ancient and medieval political thinkers did not have much use for the idea of representation. They tended to see top-down and bottom-up politics as mutually antagonistic and imagined that the character of every political society depended on the distribution of power between them: the rulers vs. the ruled, the rich vs. the poor, the elite vs. the mass, the king vs. the citizenry. Politics was, always and endlessly, the few against the many, the many against the few. The only hope for stability lay in some kind of balance between these competing elements in political life: that, for instance, was Aristotle's view. But political balance was a precarious business. It was always in danger of breaking down. For that reason Hobbes hated the idea of balance; he hated distributions of power between the different elements of society; and he hated Aristotle. Representation said goodbye to all that. It meant you didn't have to choose. In fact, it meant you couldn't choose. Either you had government and people together, or you had neither.

We now think that representation *means* political choice. We have come to associate it with the idea of democracy: we use elections to choose our representatives, and if we don't like the choice we made we use elections to get rid of them. Hobbes was extremely wary of democracy, suspecting that it would prove too contentious and destabilising in the long run. He was wrong about that. But at the basis of Hobbes's philosophy lies a democratic idea: the thought that people must agree to be represented if politics is to work at all. Once that agreement is secure, then the space is cleared for peaceful co-existence. In that space all sorts of things are possible. One of the things that might be possible is an extended experiment with greater democracy. It is not inconsistent with Hobbes's political philosophy to think that representative government could open the door to more consensual and interactive forms of politics, such as the ones we have today. He just wanted us to remember that having a nicer government was always predicated on the agreement to be governed, never the other way round. He was not wrong about that.

Making the move into the Hobbesian world of politics is not all bread and roses. It comes at a cost. It means giving up on grander political visions, including all the ones that suppose politics can make us better people. It dumps the possibility of political virtue for the sake of political security. It closes off politics as the path to other-worldly rewards. Many have found modern politics frustrating for these reasons and have railed against it. Many still do. But most of us seem broadly to accept it, especially once political stability has proved its worth by greatly enhancing our prosperity. Hobbesian politics, even when it's been democratised, tends

to produce unengaged, unadventurous, crabby citizens who accept politics as a fact of life but don't expect too much from it. They look for adventure elsewhere. They rarely come together to make big decisions. In fact, on Hobbes's account, they only do that when their fundamental safety is at risk, which is never pleasant and best avoided. Hobbesian citizens prefer to take their chances outside politics. I think we can recognise something of ourselves in this picture, however much we may dislike it. Our political world is very different from the one that Hobbes found himself living in. But it is still Hobbes's world.

THE DILEMMA OF DIRTY HANDS

There is one question that Hobbes did not fully answer. What's it like to *be* the sovereign? How does it feel to be the one who actually has all that power? Mostly he was writing about what it's like to live under a sovereign (basic message: it could always be a lot worse). But there is enough in Hobbes to suggest that being a sovereign is never going to be easy. It is a double role. Yes, you have fearsome power, including the power to use unassailable violence, which you will need to stop troublemakers from backsliding into civil disorder. At the same time, though, you are meant to be calming things down: your job is to create the ground rules for peace. You are supposed to be reliable as well as terrifying, familiar as well as remote, different from everyone else and yet no different from anyone else. (The power you have is made up of the power they would have if they hadn't handed it over to you.) You can't claim to be anyone special, certainly not hand-picked by God. You will be judged not by who you are but by what you do, but you can only do what you do because of who you are. It's a schizophrenic task. It's easy to see how it could make anyone a little crazy.

How to be bad and good at the same time is a fundamental challenge of modern politics. The bad is the threat of violence. The good is using it well, to make things better. But how can threats of violence make things better? Hobbes provided one answer. Another, different sort of answer comes from an earlier thinker, who is often identified as the true founder of modern politics. Machiavelli's *The Prince* was written in 1513, and it has haunted the Western political imagination ever since. If 'Hobbesian' has come to mean a violent free-for-all, 'Machiavellian' has come to mean the unscrupulous and devious pursuit of power for its own sake. Machiavelli is seen as the arch-exponent of what later became known as 'realpolitik': the idea that a political act is justified if it works to the advantage of the person who performs it. In these terms, it is easy to see how the threat of violence can do good: it just has to make you better off than the person on the receiving end. The blunt implication is that any other notion of 'good' is for losers.

'Machiavellian' in this sense is a caricature of Machiavelli, just as 'Hobbesian' is a caricature of Hobbes. Machiavelli was really a kind of moralist. However, the morality he had in mind was a distinctively political morality. He was satirising the idea of Christian virtue and the assumption that rulers should be in the business of justifying their rule in the eyes of God. Like Hobbes, he thought that politics had to be justified in its own terms. Unlike Hobbes, he saw the problem from the point of view of the people doing the ruling, not those being ruled. For Machiavelli, the job of ruling was to maintain your estate: that is, to preserve intact the domain over which your power runs. The purpose was not just survival; it was also glory. To master a domain is to be master of one's fate. It meant being alive to the role of chance in politics.

No ruler survives who discounts the unexpected hazards that can appear out of a clear blue sky. Danger can come from anywhere. Christian virtue is no protection

against nasty surprises. If you turn the other cheek, you'll just get hit from the other side. A ruler must use his power to preserve it: divide his enemies, probe for weaknesses, seize the moment; lie, flatter and deceive if necessary; but always make sure that others are more afraid of what he can do to them than he is of what they can do to him. As Machiavelli famously said, it is better to be feared than to be loved. If you can manage to appear lovable while still being feared, that is even better.

Machiavelli calls this sort of behaviour 'virtuous'. It *is* good, he insists. It's just not good by conventional standards. It is good by political standards. The idea that politics has its own code of conduct that is separate from conventional morality is a distinctively modern one. It makes politics a separate sphere of life rather than an exemplification of how to live. It means politicians can't be expected to set a good example. It allows them to be worse people than us by our standards, but better people than us by their standards. What they are better at is politics.

The Prince was written for the seething and precarious world of early sixteenth-century Italian politics, where a knife in the back – or more likely a vial of poison – was never far away. This was the age of the Borgias. It was also the age of fragile and violent city-states like Lucca. But high politics everywhere has its Machiavellian side, even in nice contemporary Denmark. One of the Danish TV programmes that has turned into a successful export is *Borgen*, a drama set in and around the office of the new prime minister, who happens to be a woman (just as, at the time of writing, the real Danish prime minister also happens to be a woman, Helle Thorning-Schmidt). *Borgen* doesn't hit the spot simply by making Danish politics seem nice – no one would watch that. What viewers also enjoy is the intrigue: the scheming, the back-stabbing, the betrayals, the seething resentments. *Borgen* shows civilised and decent Danish politicians doing whatever it takes, first to their enemies and then to their friends, to maintain their power. In this they are egged on by their advisers, whose main job is to ensure that their bosses don't relapse into niceness at moments of weakness. In a key early scene, the new prime minister is taken to the top of the parliament building by her mentor, who shows her Copenhagen spread out before them. This is yours, he says, if you want it. But you have to want it. She is a nice woman. But she is also a politician. Chastened, she goes back down and reconvenes the meeting she had just abandoned in tears. This time she gets her way, with smiling threats and outright lies. It is a Machiavellian moment.

The darker parts of *Borgen* describe a way of doing politics that would be entirely familiar at the court of Assad in Syria, as they would anywhere that people compete for power. Politicians the world over can read *The Prince* and see something of themselves in it. The stakes are not the same everywhere – in some systems politicians are still playing for their lives, whereas in others the losers get to retire on comfortable pensions – but the game is the same. It's a fight to reach the top and stay there. Of course, people play this game outside of politics too: in business, in the arts, in academic life, in sport. But politics is still the definitive version of the game. The Liverpool manager Bill Shankly once joked that football's not a matter of life and death: it's more important than that. Politics *is* a matter of life and death. It's precisely as important as that, even in Denmark, where politicians may not kill each other any more but innocents still die as a result of their grubby deals. A pension cut that helps keep a government in power also guarantees that a few more old people won't survive the winter. The prize for winning in politics is qualitatively different from other spheres of life. If you win in football, you get money and a trophy; if you win in the arts, you get money and kudos; if you win in business, you get money and more money. If you win in politics, you might not get the money but you do get to make the rules for everyone else. That's a prize worth fighting for. It's also a prize that encourages politicians to think that the normal rules don't apply to them.

Machiavellianism is not hard to find in modern politics. But in one crucial respect Machiavelli remains a pre-modern thinker. The first line of *The Prince*, which most readers barely notice, is the giveaway: 'ALL STATES, all powers that have held and hold rule over men have been and are either republics or principalities.' Machiavelli still belongs to the either/or world where politics is *either* kingly politics *or* citizen politics, in which power resides *either* in a single set of hands *or* in many hands. Machiavelli wrote another guide to politics after *The Prince*, this time for republics, which drew on the historical experience of ancient Rome. *The Discourses* spells out some of the same lessons as *The Prince*, especially about being alive to the role of chance. It also makes clear that, if citizens want to maintain *their* power, they will have to use it against their enemies. But Machiavelli would never have thought that a republic and a principality should be confused with each other: they were practically opposites, not least because the people who ruled them were invariably opposed to each other.

Now, if you live in a modern representative democracy, ask yourself: is it a republic or a principality? The answer is that it is neither because it is both, and it is both because it is neither. This is what Hobbes did: he abolished the distinction. Even the United States, which calls itself a republic, has what appears to be a prince in its president, as well as what seems like a princely court in the schemers around him. Elites, especially moneyed elites, are far too powerful in America for it to count as a Machiavellian republic. But Obama is not really a prince, because his power is heavily circumscribed by popular politics. He still depends on the authorisation of ordinary citizens and their representatives. There are significant constitutional limits to what he can do with his power: he can't treat it as his personal property. His job is not to maintain his estate. It's to represent the United States of America.

Modern politics combines extraordinary personal power on the part of its leading politicians with the impersonal institutional apparatus of a state. This creates a distinctive moral and psychological dynamic that goes beyond Machiavelli. It is best described as 'Weberian', after the early twentieth-century German sociologist Max Weber. It is from Weber that we have what has become the most famous definition of a modern state: 'That entity which successfully claims a monopoly of the legitimate use of violence.' The words that leap out from this definition are 'monopoly' and 'violence', but they aren't the really important ones. What the state claims is a monopoly of 'legitimate' violence: i.e., violence with no comeback. Moreover, it is only a 'claim', not a fact. What it needs to be is 'successful', meaning that people must accept it. When that happens, an 'entity' or institution is created whose power will be greater than that of any individual, though it will still be individuals who exercise its power. This is a thoroughly Hobbesian definition of the state.

What Weber saw is that the existence of these entities changes the character of political violence. They don't abolish it. What they do is institutionalise, rationalise and bureaucratise it. Successful states, in controlling violence, build up a network of institutions whose job is to manage it. There are rules, guidelines, protocols and chains of command. Politicians find themselves surrounded by civil servants and legal officers warning them of the risks and the caveats that apply to the use of force. Yet ultimately decisions about when to use force must rest with the politicians. They are still the only people who can declare war on external enemies; they are the only people who can call in the police on internal ones.

Weber's fear was that this would encourage politicians to be irresponsible in their use of violence. He meant two things by this. One form of irresponsibility is to shy away from violence altogether, in the hope that politics can do without it. Politicians might start to believe that politics is a reasonable, rule-governed, morally acceptable activity. It isn't. Sometimes politicians have to do nasty things

MAX WEBER

because every state will face real threats to its peace and security. The people who always play by the rules are either saints or bureaucrats, and Weber was adamant that both saints and bureaucrats make bad politicians. (He thought the professions that made the best politicians were lawyers and journalists, since their members are used to twisting the rules to suit their own purposes.)

The other form of irresponsibility, however, is to over-indulge in violence, on the grounds that the politician is not performing the violence him- or herself. It is being done in the name of the state, for some higher purpose that transcends mere individual responsibility. Politicians who think like this can end up wallowing in violence since they do not personally have to face the consequences: it is their decision but it's not their violence, because the machinery of the state does all the dirty work. Weber wanted politicians to remember that if it's their decision, it *is* their violence. Politicians can't evade responsibility for the nasty stuff they do by pleading politics, even though it was politics that made them do it.

This is the dilemma of 'dirty hands'. Politics is impossible if you aren't willing to get your hands dirty, but if you think that politics justifies whatever dirt you pick up, then you're liable to end up elbow-deep in blood. How can we allow politicians to do harm without encouraging them to think that the harm they do doesn't matter? Weber had no real solution to this dilemma. He insisted that politicians had to hold themselves personally responsible for their dirty deeds, but it's not clear what that means: is feeling bad about doing bad really enough? At the very least, he thought that anyone who wants to be a leader in a modern state should be alive to the ethical difficulties. You will sometimes have to be bad to do good. At the same time, you shouldn't think that the good ever absolves you of the bad. Weber called it dealing with the devil (Machiavelli never said that, which led some to think *he* must be the devil). The personal strain of holding yourself together under such diabolical pressures might send many of us mad, which is why Weber thought politics was not for most people. It was for politicians.

Weber was grappling with these questions at a particularly violent time. In the immediate aftermath of the First World War, Germany stood on the brink of civil war. Weber saw Bolshevik revolutionaries on the left and proto-fascist paramilitaries on the right glorifying violence as a force for good in a wicked world: he thought these wannabe politicians were self-deluded and deeply irresponsible. At the same time he feared that the democratic leaders of the new Weimar Republic would be too squeamish to stand up to them: in the hope of saving the integrity of their shiny new state they would abjure the hard decisions that might preserve it. The wrong people were wallowing in violence while the right people were running scared of it. Political catastrophe loomed.

In the short run, Weber's fears were overblown. (He died in 1920, and the Weimar Republic survived him.) In the longer run, however, he was right to be so worried. (The Weimar Republic eventually died in 1933, and we all know what came next.) When it came to the crunch, German democracy did not know how to defend itself, with calamitous consequences. Yet many contemporary democracies are far removed from these kinds of terrors. Weber was contemplating the collapse of civil order and the destruction of his country: 'the polar night of icy darkness', as he called it. Violence was everywhere in the final years of his life and threatening to run out of control. In that respect, he was closer to the world Hobbes knew than he is to ours. These days there are few safer places in the world to find yourself than Germany, a peaceful, stable, law-abiding democracy. And when politics is safer, we are able to expect our politicians to be nicer. Weber can seem like he belongs to another, nastier age.

But the dilemma of dirty hands has not gone away, and not only in those parts of our world that still resemble post-First-World-War Germany. (Post-Mubarak Egypt is one, post-Saddam Iraq is another.) Even nice, law-abiding politicians still find themselves doing the nastiest things. The current Obama administration has ramped up the use of drone warfare in response to the threat that terrorism continues to pose to the security of the American state. The rationale is straightforward: drones kill, but in killing they save lives. They can be targeted directly at the bad guys, who can be taken out without the lives of American soldiers being put at risk. But even twenty-first-century technology doesn't ensure that only the bad guys die or that the right bad guys are always the targets. Rockets sometimes misfire, and targets sometimes get misidentified. Collateral damage is unavoidable: innocents will also die, including children. On occasion American citizens may find themselves in the firing line. Drone warfare is still a horribly dirty business. There will be lots of blood.

An American president who refused even to contemplate using drone technology on the grounds that people might die would be, as Weber has it, no sort of politician. Politicians do sometimes have to kill people to save lives. But that in itself doesn't justify the use of drones. There are

enormous risks to this kind of streamlined, remote-controlled violence. One is that it appears sanitised: it tempts politicians into thinking that they have chosen the safe option and to forget that even the safe option is hideously unpleasant for the people on the receiving end. It can also be excessively rationalised: the immediate calculus of lives lost to lives saved is only one consideration in a messy and complex situation. Efficient, cost-effective killing machines encourage a bureaucratic mindset to take hold at the expense of political judgement. (Another group that Weber thought ill qualified to be politicians were professional soldiers: they were too used to thinking of violence in terms

of its efficiency.) Whenever political violence is deployed, there is more than just its cost-effectiveness to consider. What about America's long-term reputation? What about the resentments that build up over time and produce uncontrolled violence much further down the line? What about the collateral damage to America's allies? Even Danes have not been immune to the fall-out: Danish politicians have not sent armed drones out into the world, but they have been tasked with providing some of the intelligence that helps identify the targets for these strikes. The rationalisation of violence spreads insidiously. Responsibility is parcelled out until no one is in a position to say no.

What might it mean to take responsibility for a drone strike? Obama can say that he agonises about it, that he feels the death of every innocent, that he never reaches such a decision lightly. But in the end it's his call, and he must judge what's best for America. Yet how different is this from washing his hands of personal responsibility? We have to take it on trust that he feels bad about it. But is feeling bad about it enough to make it all right? The problem goes beyond mere Machiavellianism, because so many different moral considerations are in play. It's a moral fudge, the one Weber warned was inevitable. The fact that it's inevitable can become its own excuse for political irresponsibility. 'Look,' the politician says, 'I know politics is the devil's business, just like Weber said. I worry about it all the time. I'm not a monster. I hate this stuff. But someone has to do it and it happens to be me. I don't sleep at night so you can sleep at night. Is that good enough?'

The answer is no: it's not good enough. It's not just the

politician's call. Weber was over-enamoured of the solitary, tragic political hero at a time when politics was often tragic and seemed to be calling out for heroes. In the early twenty-first century the balance of risk has changed. Civil disorder is not always the number one danger. There are also the threats to the shared principles of political conduct that stable politics has made possible. Politicians have responsibilities not only to their own citizens but also to constitutional proprieties, to international law and to global public opinion. These all impose constraints that they ignore at their and our peril. Politicians can't simply be accountable to their consciences. Someone or something else must also hold them to account.

THE PERILS OF PEACE

But who is going to do it? Stable politics poses a moral challenge to citizens as much as it does to politicians. We too can become squeamish about violence, knowing that someone else is taking care of it. We focus on our own lives and material comforts and turn a blind eye to the nasty stuff. Drone warfare suits an age in which people prefer not to engage with the most difficult political questions: out of sight, out of mind. Can politicians be blamed if they exploit the leeway we give them to do it the way that suits them best?

The danger of modern politics is that stability produces disengagement. Citizens who are protected from the most destabilising threats of violence start to lose interest in politics altogether: it becomes the background noise in their lives. But violence never goes away entirely. Instead it gets franchised out to government agencies who take advantage of our inattention to abuse the power we give them. They do it because they can. So the unintended consequence of the control of violence is that we allow violence to run out of our control.

The thinker who saw this paradoxical feature of modern political life most clearly was Benjamin Constant, a French-Swiss romantic, novelist, constitutional theorist and intermittent politician. Constant lived two hundred years ago, and he enjoyed the benefits of modern life and the freedoms it offered, including the freedom to follow your heart (like many romantics, he fell in love with the idea of falling in love).

Constant lived through the French Revolution and the Terror that followed (though, as with Hobbes during the English civil war, he survived it by making sure he wasn't around for the worst bits – he went to Germany), then the rise and fall of Napoleon and the subsequent restoration of the French monarchy. So he also saw the downside of modern politics: its capacity to wreak havoc when it went wrong. What made him unusual was that he believed the two things were connected: the pleasures of modernity and its dangers. People who concentrate on their private satisfactions leave themselves vulnerable to spasmodic outbreaks of uncontrolled violence. Why? Because if everyone is busy following his or her heart, no one is keeping an eye on what the politicians are doing.

Constant gave a famous lecture in 1819 in which he compared ancient to modern political liberty. In the ancient world citizens were required to participate in politics as the focal point of their existence and the bedrock of their freedom. They could hardly ignore the threat of violence: it was everywhere in societies that were built on slavery and organised to fight endless wars. Peace was the rare exception, not the rule. Modern citizens, if they are lucky, can forget about violence and learn to downplay the importance of politics. Constant acknowledged that the Hobbesian idea of representative government lay at the root of the transition. But he thought Hobbes had only got it half right. Hobbes had understood the need to franchise out political decision-making but had neglected the risks of giving all that power to a single authority. Constant believed in the constitutional separation of powers. The key to stable politics was to give the separate branches of government – executive, legislature and judiciary – the right to represent the state in their different capacities. In this way politicians could keep an eye on each other. This was the idea that lay behind the new American republic that had come into existence at the end of the eighteenth century. Constant wanted it for France.

However, it could not be the whole answer. If politicians were keeping an eye on each other, who was keeping an eye on the politicians? A moderated Hobbesian state, organised around a well-designed constitution, was dangerous because it allowed people to forget what underpinned their security. (That's one reason why Hobbes would have been suspicious of it.) When peace becomes the rule and war the rare exception, it is easy to drift into thinking politics has little bearing on everyday life. Constant foresaw two risks. One was that politicians would hive off secret networks of coercive power which they could use for their own purposes. Their divided interest in checking on each other would lose out to their shared interest in keeping the public in the dark. This is how little states within the state arise: pockets of wealth, privilege and paranoia that know to give each other a wide berth.

The other risk was that the public would occasionally wake up to its political passivity and lash out. People who lose interest in politics don't give up on politics entirely. Instead they become sullen, resentful and prone to fantasies of revenge. They fall prey to provocateurs peddling stories of political transformation. Constant thought one such story had taken hold in France before the revolution: the ideal of ancient politics where citizens were able to control their own destiny. Look how powerless you have become, went the refrain; then look at the ancients, the heroic Greeks and the noble Romans. That was how to live (so long as you weren't a slave, or a woman or anyone with a private life). Take back the power! Result: chaos. Fantasies of a rebirth of pure political liberty had led to the uncontrolled violence of the revolution.

Modern politics was a balancing act. Expecting too much participation was unsustainable in large, diverse commercial societies such as nineteenth-century France. (In which case, how much more so today.) People simply didn't have the time or the inclination to get involved, which meant that, if you wanted them all to take part, you ended up having to force them to participate with threats of violence. Guillotines do not make good citizens, just frightened or dead ones. But allowing too little participation opened up a dangerous gap between citizens and their governments. Bad government would be the inevitable result of the public's inattention. Constant's answer was vigilance without total immersion. He wanted citizens to be better-informed about politics, to read the newspapers and debate the issues, to join clubs and political parties, to petition their representatives to keep them on their toes. There ought to be time to do this while still leaving plenty of room for private satisfactions. A partly political life is perhaps not as much fun as a purely private life. But in the end there is no such thing as a purely private life. The avoidance of politics leaves anyone vulnerable to being swallowed up by politics without warning.

Leading a partly political life is never easy, however. There are so many distractions. Newspapers don't just report on what the politicians are getting up to. There is also sport, and art, and money, and travel, and celebrity, and sex. (Constant was keen on all these things, bar the first; he was keen on religion instead.) The internet makes it much worse: even if you wanted to inform yourself about politics, it's so hard to know where to start and when to stop. There is too much information and not enough time. We are still caught in the bind Constant identified. Political parties are dying, newspapers are disappearing and our political attention spans are spasmodic and haphazard at best. We allow government to drift away from us and then, when we discover that pockets of wealth and power and privilege have grown up unchecked, we lash out.

The fantasy of ancient politics doesn't have much pull any more. But other fantasies have taken its place: the anarchist fantasies of Occupy Wall Street, the originalist fantasies of the Tea Party movement. The prospect of revolution is remote, but occasionally there are outbreaks of real violence. The riots that took place in Britain in the summer of 2011 were not evidence of a broken society, as the doomsters imagined. They were evidence of a distracted society: alongside the pockets of privilege are pockets of real deprivation, and between the two are vast swathes of people who have failed to pay much attention to either. The randomness of the violence and the speed with which it flared up and then burned out are typical of society in which most people are failing to live even a partly political life. Politics means too

little most of the time, and then for a few moments it means too much. Long periods of indifference interspersed with brief spasms of fury is no way to do politics.

Stable, distracted modern societies can still be very different in how they deal with these outbreaks of violence. Some are much more punitive than others. Like everywhere else, Denmark has its prisons to lock up those who do significant harm to the persons and property of the law-abiding majority. But compared with many countries, its prisons look more like hotels: comfortable rooms, TVs, computers, bright and cheerful communal spaces, conjugal visits and a strong focus on rehabilitation. There are also relatively few of them. The Danish prison population is just under 4,000 people, or around 60 for every 100,000 of the population at large. In Britain the rate is double that (and many of the rioters in 2011 faced long custodial sentences). In America it is massively higher still. The total number of people in jail in the United States is more than 2.2 million; in addition, another 4 million are either on probation or on parole. The rate of those in jail per 100,000 of the American population is close to 800, or 15 times the rate in Denmark. For black prisoners it is nearly 4,500 per 100,000, or 1 in every 22 people. In parts of the United States young black men are significantly more likely to be in prison than in employment. In these respects, the United States and Denmark are worlds apart. Seen through the prism of its penal system, the US looks more like Syria.

For a stable democracy, the United States remains a strikingly violent place, though there is evidence that the overall level of violence is in steady decline. (Crime rates have fallen precipitously in many American cities, as they have across the Western world.) Europeans are still shocked by the readiness with which some American citizens reach for their guns and the vehemence with which they defend their right to use them. Also shocking for many outsiders is the continuing resort to the death penalty. The United States executed 39 prisoners in 2013. The only countries to make more extensive use of capital punishment were Iraq, Iran, Saudi Arabia and China, which executes thousands every year.

So America is a punitive as well as a comparatively violent society. It is also riven by deep social and cultural disagreements about these very practices. Texas has executed more than 500 people since the death penalty was restored in 1976 (a third of whom have been black, though black Texans make up less than 12 per cent of the total population of the state). In many other states, including Maine, Massachusetts, New Hampshire, New York, Rhode Island and Vermont, not a single person has been executed over the same period. (Today just 2 per cent of American counties account for the majority of all executions.) For every American committed to gun ownership there is someone else who wants guns controlled: polls split roughly 50:50 on the question of whether the right to bear arms is more important than the right of government to regulate it.

Yet the disagreements between Americans about the instruments of violence are trumped by a long-standing agreement about how to resolve those differences. America is still much more like Denmark than it is like Syria. The proof is that the competing sides in the United States do not resort to violence to settle their political disputes, even though those disputes are passionate, intractable and often fuelled by religion. In the political contest over gun ownership, there is an obvious imbalance between the parties: one – the pro-gun lobby – has more guns than its opponents. This extends to other political divisions: Republicans are on the whole better-armed than Democrats. It ought to be a recipe for civil war. But it isn't. The minimalist definition of modern representative democracy says that it is a proxy for civil war: i.e., it is the conflict without the violence. When one side loses an election, it lets the other side take power, despite the fact that the losers possess the weapons to fight (and all defeated incumbents have weaponry to resist on election day, because they still control the army). On this account, stable politics simply requires that people with access to guns choose not to use them.

Has the threat of civil war vanished altogether in these societies? It certainly seems pretty remote, even in the United States, whose political system was only secured in the nineteenth century by one of the most terrible civil wars in history. The 2000 presidential election that resulted in an effective tie between Al Gore and George W. Bush provoked a furious political disagreement about who the real winner was. Some excitable journalists started to wonder whether violence would be needed to settle the outcome. Instead, it was settled by the Supreme Court (though it helped that the court decided in favour of the candidate whose supporters were more likely to be armed). The decision was a brazenly political one, but the losers accepted it. They concluded that their best option was to wait to get their revenge at the ballot box, which they did in 2008. A civil war was never really on the cards.

There is significant empirical evidence that once societies reach a certain level of material prosperity – usually estimated at around $6,000 per capita GDP – democratic political institutions are very unlikely to be challenged by force. However much citizens in these societies may dislike the results of an election, they dislike even more the prospect of violent disruption to their peaceful lives. This threshold has only been passed relatively recently in many places that now look very stable. New Zealand, for instance, fell perilously close to it during the global recession of the 1970s. It seems hard to imagine a violent coup in 1970s' New Zealand, but it's not impossible. There were regular mutterings in Britain about the army having to take over during the dark days of the mid-1970s, though in retrospect the threat seems slightly farcical. (The plots we know about planned to install Lord Mountbatten as a de facto head of the government, which is more P. G. Wodehouse than *Mein Kampf.*) Per capita GDP in Britain in 1970 was around $10,000. Today it is $38,000. Even in present-day Greece, despite the vicious contraction of the Greek economy since 2008, per capita GDP is around $21,000 (a decline of nearly a third since its peak five years earlier). Greece is a society in deep trouble, with nasty pockets of violence. But it is a long way from civil war.

So are we safe? It would be complacent to think so. The problem stable political societies face in the twenty-first century is that we don't know what failure is going to look like. There are simply no historical precedents to go on: we have no examples of prosperous, secure, successful societies, used to the levels of comfort and material benefits of today's Western democracies, going into reverse. That doesn't mean

it can't happen. It is easy to conjure up apocalyptic scenarios, such as the one portrayed in Cormac McCarthy's novel *The Road*, where an unspecified disaster reduces the United States to something even worse than the Hobbesian state of nature, complete with terrifying violence, utter lawlessness and cannibalism. (The film version was shot in parts of Pittsburgh, though by most accounts Pittsburgh is not such a bad place to live these days.) Much harder is to imagine what non-apocalyptic failure is likely to entail. This is the irony of the world Hobbes created. The success of the Hobbesian project – our emancipation not only from the state of nature but also from the threat of civil war – means that we don't really know what the alternatives are.

BANG

STABLE? DID SOMEBODY MENTION STABLES?

CTABLE UNSTABLE

POLITICS

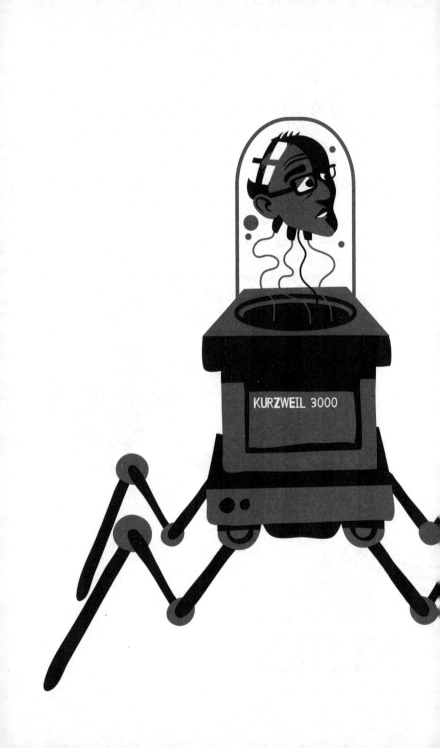

2
TECHNOLOGY

THE TECHNOLOGY REVOLUTION

Civil wars are always bad. Revolutions can be good (though my revolution might be your civil war). The political transition from insecurity to stability often requires a violent kick-start to get it going. Failed regimes do not usually give up without a fight; power needs to be dragged from them by force. Most of the epochal events that signalled the arrival of modern politics have been revolutions, some of them more violent than others: the Glorious Revolution of 1688, which was not so glorious for the thousands who lost their lives (especially in Ireland); the American Revolution of 1776, which turned out to be a bloody war of attrition; the French Revolution of 1789, which produced real carnage but still retains its appeal as the ultimate symbol of emancipatory politics, and not just for the French. Nothing can match the blood-quickening drama of a people seizing power from a king, storming his prisons and palaces and, if necessary, cutting off his head.

Subsequent revolutions have complicated this picture. The revolutions that swept Europe in 1848 promised to usher in a new age of democracy, which they eventually did, but only many decades later. The revolutions themselves petered out into almost nothing, thanks to political infighting and military repression. The great communist revolutions of the twentieth century are increasingly difficult to valorise on any grounds. Russia 1917 and China 1949 were transformative events. But the human cost of the regimes they brought into being is indefensible. All too often, revolutions produce more violence, not less, and create political conditions that are hard to distinguish from civil war. The Arab Spring of 2011 was a profoundly hopeful event. Plenty of comparisons were made at the time to 1776 or 1789 or even 1917 (though more far-sighted commentators compared it to 1848). Two years on, mounting chaos in Syria, Libya and Egypt has dampened the enthusiasm almost everywhere, as hope gives way to fear. There are good reasons to be wary of revolutions.

Despite this, it would be a mistake to think the age of political revolution is over. It is far too soon to tell what the ultimate fate of the Arab Spring will be. In the meantime, who knows what might happen in other parts of the world, including in China. And we should not forget that we are still only a generation away from perhaps the most successful and peaceful revolutions of modern times: the popular uprisings of 1989 that swept away the discredited and bankrupted communist regimes of Eastern Europe. Dramatic political change is still possible.

However, it does not follow that dramatic change is always political. There are other kinds of revolution. The most significant revolution of the twenty-first century so far is not political. It is the information technology revolution. Its transformative effects are everywhere. In many places rapid technological change stands in stark contrast to the lack of political change.

Take the United States. Its political system has hardly changed at all since 1989. Even the moments of apparent transformation – such as the election of Obama in 2008 – have only reinforced how entrenched the established order is: once the excitement died away, Obama was left facing the same constrained political choices. American politics is stuck in a rut. But the lives of American citizens have been revolutionised over the same period. The birth of the web and the development of cheap and efficient devices through which to access it have completely altered the way people connect with each other. Vast amounts of information have become readily accessible to anyone who wants it; the speed of communication has increased exponentially, and physical distance has shrunk accordingly; networks of people with shared interests, tastes, concerns, fetishes, prejudices and fears have sprung up in limitless varieties. The information technology revolution has changed the way human beings befriend each other, how they meet, date, communicate, medicate, investigate, negotiate and decide who they want to be and what they want to do. Many aspects of our online world would be unrecognisable to someone who was transplanted here from any point in the twentieth century. But the infighting and gridlock in Washington would be all too familiar.

This isn't just an American story. China hasn't changed much politically since 1989, when the massacre in Tiananmen Square snuffed out a would-be revolution and secured the hold on power of the current regime. But China itself is a totally altered place since then. Economic growth is a large part of the difference. But so is the revolution in technology. A country of more than a billion people, nearly half of whom still live in the countryside, has been transformed by the mobile phone. There are currently over a billion phones in use in China. Ten years ago fewer than one in ten Chinese had access to one; today there is nearly one per person. Individuals whose horizons were until very recently constrained by physical geography – to live and die within a radius of a few miles from your birthplace was not unusual for Chinese peasants even into this century – now have access to the wider world. For the present, though maybe not for much longer, the spread of new technology has helped to stifle the call for greater political change. Who needs a political revolution when you've got a technological one?

Technology has the power to make politics seem obsolete. The speed of change leaves government looking slow, cumbersome, unwieldy and often irrelevant. It can also make political thinking look tame by comparison with the big ideas coming out of the tech industry. This doesn't just apply to far-out ideas about what will soon be technologically possible: intelligent robots, computer implants in the human brain, virtual reality that is indistinguishable from 'real' reality (all things that Ray Kurzweil, co-founder of the Google-sponsored Singularity University, thinks are coming by 2030). In this post-ideological age some of the most exotic political visions are the ones that emerge from discussions about tech. You'll find more radical libertarians and outright communists among computer scientists than among political scientists. Advances in computing have thrown up fresh ways to think about what it means to own something, what it means to share something and what it means to have a private life at all. These are among the basic questions of modern politics. However, the new answers rarely get expressed in political terms (with the exception of heated debates about civil rights for robots). More often they are expressions of frustration with politics and sometimes of outright contempt for it. Technology isn't seen as a way of doing politics better. It's seen as a way of bypassing politics altogether.

In some circumstances, technology can and should bypass politics. The advent of widespread mobile phone ownership has allowed some of the world's poorest citizens to wriggle free from the trap of failed government. In countries that lack basic infrastructure – an accessible transport network, a reliable legal system, a usable banking sector – phones enable people to create their own networks of ownership and exchange. In Africa a grassroots, phone-based banking system has sprung up that for the first time permits money transfers without the physical exchange of cash. This makes it possible for the inhabitants of desperately poor and isolated rural areas to do business outside of their local communities. Technology caused this to happen; government didn't. For many Africans phones are an escape route from the constrained existence that bad politics has for so long mired them in.

But it would be a mistake to overstate what phones can do. They won't rescue anyone from civil war. Africans can use their phones to tell the wider world of the horrors that are still taking place in some parts of the continent – in

South Sudan, in Eritrea, in the Niger Delta, in the Central African Republic, in Somalia. Unfortunately the world does not often listen, and nor do the soldiers who are doing the killing. Phones have not changed the basic equation of political security: the people with the guns need a compelling reason not to use them. Technology by itself doesn't give them that reason. Equally, technology by itself won't provide the basic infrastructure whose lack it has provided a way around. If there are no functioning roads to get you to market, a phone is godsend when you have something to sell. But in the long run, you still need the roads. Everything will go better with them. Government is needed to build

and maintain roads, especially to poor and isolated areas that lack the means to pay for them. Government upholds the rule of law. Government secures property rights. The consequences of state failure can sometimes be ameliorated by technological fixes, but they can't be remedied by them. For that, you need well-functioning states. In the end, only politics can rescue you from bad politics.

In the developed world, impatience with politics takes another form. We don't look to technology to rescue us from failed states. We look to it to rescue us from overbearing ones. Politics in the West can appear bloated and stale. This is especially true of the large, complex and inflexible welfare

THE SIX EPOCHS OF EVOLUTION

EVOLUTION WORKS THROUGH INDIRECTION: IT CREATES A CAPABILITY AND THEN USES THAT CAPABILITY TO EVOLVE TO THE NEXT STAGE

VASTLY EXPANDED HUMAN INTELLIGENCE (PREDOMINANTLY NONBIOLOGICAL) SPREADS THROUGH THE UNIVERSE

TECHNOLOGY MASTERS METHODS OF BIOLOGY (INCLUDING HUMAN INTELLIGENCE)

NOLOGY
VES

EPOCH 6 THE UNIVERSE WAKES UP
PATTERNS OF MATTER & ENERGY IN THE UNIVERSE BECOME SATURATED WITH INTELLIGENT PROCESSES & KNOWLEDGE

EPOCH 5 MERGER OF TECHNOLOGY & HUMAN INTELLIGENCE
THE METHODS OF BIOLOGY (INCLUDING HUMAN INTELLIGENCE) ARE INTEGRATED INTO THE (EXPONENTIALLY EXPANDING) HUMAN TECHNOLOGY BASE

EPOCH 4 TECHNOLOGY
INFORMATION IN HARDWARE & SOFTWARE DESIGNS

EPOCH 3 BRAINS
INFORMATION IN NEURAL PATTERNS

EPOCH 2 BIOLOGY
INFORMATION IN DNA

EPOCH 1 PHYSICS & CHEMISTRY
INFORMATION IN ATOMIC STRUCTURES

RAY KURZWEIL

systems that have grown up since the Second World War. It has become easy to associate politics with entrenched interests and stifling bureaucracy. It is tempting to blame these for the rising burden of debt faced by many democratic countries. By contrast, the tech world looks dynamic, flexible and exciting. It invents new stuff all the time. It is relentless in its search for what works, unencumbered by sterile political mindsets. When did a government last create anything as beneficial for the public welfare as Wikipedia? When did a bureaucracy ever invent anything as life-enhancing as Google?

It can be painful watching democratic politicians attempt to play catch-up with the new technology. They know they need to try, but often they don't know how. A few politicians have worked out how to use Twitter effectively, but most only get the public's attention when they discover new ways to make fools of themselves. The track record of many government bureaucracies in making best use of the new technology is lamentable. More tax-payers' money in Britain has been wasted on mismanaged IT projects in recent years than on anything else, including mismanaged wars (and the cost of these is driven inexorably higher by the wasteful expenditure of the military on high-tech systems that turn out to be less efficient than the ones they replaced). There have been countless local experiments around the world in how to use the internet to promote more accountable and efficient government: online town hall meetings, interactive consultation exercises, micro referendums. The trouble comes in knowing how to filter the results, learn from them and then scale them up. Government is not much good at any of this: it fails to pick up on what works, in time to take advantage of it.

These failures help breed contempt for politicians not only among citizens but within from the tech industry, which often assumes that government is simply an obstacle to be overcome: an analogue annoyance in a digital world. But there are some things the tech industry doesn't understand very well. Its blind spots include the story of its own origins. There would be no tech industry on the scale we know it today without government. This is not simply because every industry needs stable and reliable political institutions to uphold the property rights on which its dynamism depends. (Tech giants are hardly less litigious than previous industrialists, and some of them, in their voracious appetite to buy up and protect patents, are as litigious as anyone in history.) It is because government investment is what made the information technology revolution possible in the first place. The historical evidence shows that really big technological change requires vast amounts of waste. Someone has to be willing to throw huge sums of money around, knowing that most of it will be money down the drain. Private investors lack the appetite for this sort of risk. Only government is willing to waste resources on such a scale. The reason is that government sometimes has more important things to worry about than squandering money. Government waste is driven by the threat of violence.

The foundations of the information technology revolution were laid during the Cold War. It has its roots in the massive US government research and development programmes of the 1950s and 1960s. During this period most of the money spent on scientific research in the United States came out of the military budget. That spending was fuelled by Cold War paranoia – we've got to out-invent those crazy, ruthless Russians! – and it was enormously wasteful. But it was what made the difference. The internet began life as a military project; so too did text messaging. Of course, government didn't know what to do with these things it had created. (The US military assumed that texting would have only very limited, exclusively military, uses.) The whizz kids of the tech industry had to step in and turn scientific innovation into marketable products: from MILNET and ARPANET to Google and Twitter. Private companies do that sort of thing much better than government does. But private companies can only do it because of the heavy lifting that's already been done by government, spending the public's money like there was no tomorrow.

The same story can be told about 'fracking', another transformative technology that is enriching plenty of private individuals who can claim to be supplying a public good (cheaper fuel). Whether or not it is a public good remains debatable: the environmental costs have yet to be reckoned. What is much harder to claim is that the people making the money are the ones responsible for the technology itself. The crucial innovations were a consequence of large-scale government spending on new means of energy extraction during the 1970s. The driving force behind that spending was the decade's 'oil crisis', starting with the Arab–Israeli war of 1973, which triggered a quadrupling of oil prices and a worldwide recession. Politicians were terrified of the possible consequences of oil scarcity: civil unrest, military weakness, social breakdown. Frightened politicians promote technological revolutions to forestall political ones. Further down the line, private investors reap the rewards.

Unfortunately, 'fracking' doesn't herald the advent of a green technological revolution. It is simply a more efficient way of extracting hard-to-get-at fossil fuels. A big shift to green technology would take something extra: a fresh set of acute political threats to get the politicians spending our money on the scale needed to trigger a fresh round of innovation. For now, the politicians are more scared of other things, including the risk of running out of the public's money. (That's where being burdened with large and inflexible welfare states may be stifling innovation.)

Anyone who thinks that technological innovation driven by market forces alone will solve a problem on the scale of climate change is deluding themselves. Market players aren't willing to take big enough risks to effect the genuinely transformative changes. Only governments do that. At the moment, the one government that is investing on a significant scale in green technology is China. This spending is driven by fears of popular unrest in response to the very high current levels of pollution. In many parts of China ordinary citizens have been living with filthy water and toxic air for a long time, and there are signs that they are not prepared to put up with it for much longer. The Chinese government is worried about what some future environmental disaster might do to its hold on power. But Chinese government spending will not be enough to make the difference on its own, and for now Western governments do not face the same kind of fears. So they are holding off. Things will probably have to get worse before they have a chance to get better. As yet, climate change hasn't got politically scary enough: there needs to be a greater threat of violence. That's the truly scary thought.

GOOGLE VS. GOVERNMENT

States can do plenty of things that business organisations can't. States fight wars; Google doesn't, and not just because the company motto is 'Don't Be Evil'. Google lacks the organisational capacity and the coercive authority for war. It couldn't fight one even if it wanted to. A state – the United States – put a man on the moon, another massively costly enterprise that had all sorts of unexpected technological spin-offs. Google might like to do something as ambitious, but it wouldn't dare be so reckless with its cash. (The Apollo programme cost well over $100 billion in today's money; the space shuttle programme cost twice as much, or more than half the current net worth of Google.) States – thanks to their tax-raising powers – are able to pool resources on a scale that not even the biggest businesses could match.

But businesses can do plenty of things that states can't. Google has just come up with a self-driving car that actually works. It has married its mapping technology to its super-smart computers to produce a machine that performs a complex task far more safely than any human being could manage. Google's self-driving cars don't crash (so far). It is hard to imagine a government programme resulting in a self-driving car that doesn't crash. Governments tend to screw up complex, open-ended tasks like that. (The mission to put a man on the moon was complex, but it wasn't open-ended: it had a straightforward, hard-to-miss target in the moon itself.) Governments don't build good cars. The hopelessly inefficient and unreliable bangers turned out by the communist states of Eastern Europe – their puttering Ladas, their tin-box Trabants – are enduring testimony to that.

Most resources work best when they aren't pooled. Competition encourages diversification as well as innovation. A business like Google can draw on sufficient resources to experiment successfully with a self-driving car. But these resources are not sufficient to stifle all rival experiments. However large Google looms over Silicon Valley, a hive of independent activity still takes place in its shadow. The creation of a steady stream of transformative, life-enhancing products depends on competitive markets in which a balance has been struck between scale and diversity. Market competition produces lots of useful things that make people's lives better. States shouldn't even try to compete: they'll just mess it up.

There are limits to what markets can do, however. Champions of the free market have a tendency to extrapolate from its creative power an unjustified faith in its ability to solve any problem. Yes, private enterprise has given us the self-driving car, which may one day have the power to change the way we live. (Sit in the back, read a book, sleep, work out, make out and suddenly your daily commute becomes the best part of the day.) But that car still needs roads to drive on and rules to govern what happens there. What about the people who don't want a self-driving car, or can't afford one, or simply enjoy being behind the wheel? Who is going to manage the transition from a driven to a driverless world? Google won't do it. Government will have to.

If the self-driving car is going to become the industry norm, it will take time and it will be messy. The transport network will have to adapt, the insurance industry will have to adapt and the legal system will have to adapt (not least to decide what to do with all those people who still insist on their right to have crashes). The market may be able to

take care of some of these things over time, but it won't be able to take care of all of them, certainly not all at the same time. Change on that scale is too fractious: as Hobbes said, people have an inbuilt tendency to collide. Government needs Google to build a car that really works. Google needs government if its car is ever really going to work.

The perspective of anyone who works at Google tends to be international. The company's employees come from all over the world, and they think that their life-enhancing products should be available all over the world. One of the attractions of innovative technology is its ability to break down national borders: it spreads everywhere once it is allowed to. Meanwhile, one of the attractions of being a multinational corporation is the ability to move money across national borders, to where it can do most work (for the owners of the corporation). Google is adept at avoiding tax in the various national jurisdictions where it operates. It pays as little as it can get away with, on the grounds that it is not Google's job to fund national governments or to set their tax rates for them. Google is in the ideas business, and good ideas know no boundaries. An international perspective always makes it tempting to look down on government.

However, the road systems on which Google's self-driving car will operate are still national. They are subject to laws made by national governments, and they are paid for with taxes raised by national governments. In the United States it is even more local than this: the rules and the funding of the road network vary from state to state. Good ideas are not going to break down these boundaries on their own. If your good idea has a crash in California, the consequences will be very different from if that crash happens over the border in Mexico. An international perspective is often blind to the resolutely national basis of the lives most of us still lead. While Google is innovating and its executives are flying around the world spreading the good news, someone still needs to pay for the basic infrastructure on which its innovations will operate. That someone is invariably the governments whose taxes Google tries to avoid.

Champions of the free market argue that it could all be done much better if government would just butt out. Seen from a market perspective, the chaos of multiple different national jurisdictions is hopelessly inefficient. Globalisation promises to render those inefficiencies obsolete over time. Trade between nations will eventually bring all nations together under a single set of rules. Politics will fade out of the picture if we let commerce flourish. All it takes is the free movement of goods and peoples: the more people are at liberty to travel as they please between Mexico and California, the less it will matter where the accidents happen. That's the hope.

International commerce trumping national politics has long been the dream, from the eighteenth century onwards, when the idea of an international market economy first took off. The reality is different. In a world of existing governments, whose basic task is to protect their citizens, unfettered globalisation is politically inefficient. Citizens don't like it because it trades short-term security – the primary currency of politics – for the uncertain promise of long-term rewards. Governments don't like it because it threatens to put them out of business. From an economic point of view protectionism doesn't make much sense. Nor do closed borders. Both are economically inefficient in the long run. But both can make plenty of sense from a political perspective, and we still live in a political world.

This logic even applies to the manufacture of cars. Governments can't do it themselves, but they can subsidise others to do it for them. Some of the world's most successful car companies, including Hyundai, of South Korea, were developed thanks to decades of import bans, export subsidies and tariff protection. Left to its own devices, the international market could have sold the South Koreans better cars than the ones made by Hyundai. But it couldn't have given South Korea what it wanted, which was a stable manufacturing base for its own entry into international markets. That required state protection during the early years to fend off the market competition.

States often make a mess of subsidies: they pick the wrong businesses to back and then prop them up long after they have become monuments to inefficiency, for fear of the political consequences of allowing them to fail. What's worse, competition between state-subsidised industries can easily spill over into political conflict. During the 1930s rising protectionism in the face of economic meltdown helped to fuel international confrontation and ultimately resulted in a world war. Nonetheless, messy as it is and dangerous as it can be, state protection for emerging industries has often been crucial for national economic success. This view also dates back to the eighteenth century, when it was recognised by a few far-sighted individuals – including the founders of the new American republic, who regularly subsidised American manufacturing industry – that free markets and controlling states need each other if they are both to flourish. Markets can't do it all themselves.

Above all, markets can't correct for their own failures. Only government has the power to pool resources on the scale needed to rescue us from markets that have fundamentally broken down. The financial crash of 2008 demonstrated this beyond reasonable doubt. Financial innovation had produced a diversity of products that were bought up by large financial institutions. These products were meant to diversify risk, but they ended up concentrating it. The big banks had grown so large that the risks of a systemic crash were greatly increased, but they were not large enough to ride out the crash by themselves. In other words, they had become too big to fail, but they were going to fail anyway.

That this had been allowed to happen was itself a failure of government, since some of the responsibility lay with the people whose job it was to regulate the banking industry. But all this shows is that government regulation is necessary to ensure markets function successfully. A government bail-out was the only possible rescue once government regulation had failed to prevent the disaster. Free-market fundamentalists can argue that there was an alternative: the big banks could have been allowed to fail and the system could have been given time to correct itself without government interference. But there simply wasn't that time. Markets do correct themselves eventually. But in the meantime the world falls apart.

Complex, innovative systems are not good at big rescues because they are unable to pool their resources quickly enough. The very forces that make them innovative – their complexity and diversity – make them cumbersome and unwieldy in a crisis. States look cumbersome and unwieldy most of the time, but in a crisis they can be decisive. In late 2008 governments around the world were required to step in to rescue their banks. Some of these decisions had to be taken incredibly quickly: once Lehman Brothers went down, calamity was sometimes just hours away. Massive government intervention was needed to prevent the contagion from spreading. The Bush administration that presided over the rescue was made up of champions of the free market. Their convictions went out the window as soon as it became clear that only government had the power to salvage the situation.

The nature of that power was coercive. Only government could force failing institutions into the arms of solvent ones; only government could bend the rules to make these mergers possible; only government could require the taxpayer to stump up the money to underwrite the costs. Without its ability to coerce, no government would have had the credibility to stem the rising tide of panic. Only government has sufficient power to make its decisions stick in a crisis. That's what it's for.

And that's what makes it frightening. Its power can easily be abused. Anyone who is on the receiving end is going to feel pretty powerless. It is even possible to feel sorry for the bankers in late 2008 who were summoned by government officials to be told their fate. 'Why me?', Dick Fuld of Lehman Brothers wanted to know. 'Why do I go to the wall when others get rescued?' 'Because we've decided', came the answer, and someone had to decide. Once government decides, it's your funeral.

When time is short, as it always is in a crisis, there is no time for niceties. One way government can abuse its power, therefore, is to drag out any crisis. It can routinise its emergency decision-making and extend the reach of its coercive powers to cover more and more everyday transactions. In this, the new technology has proved an invaluable resource. It has made it much easier for government to oversee what people and institutions are up to in order to check that they are not posing an unacceptable

WHAT IT MEANS TO OWN SOMETHING

WHAT IT MEANS TO SHARE SOMETHING

WHAT IT MEANS TO HAVE A PRIVATE LIFE AT ALL

DONALD KNUTH

EDWARD SNOWDEN

GEORGE CLOONEY

risk. Government can now spy on us in all sorts of exciting new ways: read our emails, listen to our phone calls, track our text messages, access our bank accounts. Government being government, it often does this inefficiently and cack-handedly, which only makes it more frightening.

The revelation that the US government has been routinely conducting electronic surveillance on its own citizens has caused deep disquiet. Among the people who have been most disturbed are members of the tech industry. Their unease is twofold: first, techies don't like being spied on; second, they don't like not being able to prevent it. After all, it's their technology that's being abused. This puts the giants of the tech industry in a bind. They have to admit their complicity – we could have stopped it, but we didn't – or they have to admit their powerlessness – we couldn't have stopped it even if we had wanted to. Either way, it makes them look like pawns of the state.

No one likes to see politicians using technology as an instrument of control, least of all the people who invented the technology. But we have to remember the alternative to politicians controlling the tech industry: it's the tech industry controlling the politicians. Government using its monopoly power to manipulate Google is bad. But Google using its monopoly power to manipulate government would be worse. That's because corporate monopolists are even less accountable than democratic governments: there is no recourse against them if government is not there to provide it. Google squeals if government does bad stuff. Who is going to squeal when Google does bad stuff, if not government?

'So what?' the Google guys may say. Remember the company motto: we aren't evil. So you won't get bad stuff from us. We don't fight wars. We don't coerce people. We have no need to abuse our powers in the way government does. That's the wishful view. The truth is that Google has no opportunity to abuse its powers the way that government does because government is there to prevent it.

Take that barrier away – give Google the right to decide where, when and how its technology is used to spy on people – and the abuse will surely follow. And perhaps, before long, the wars as well. Who would you rather controlled your technology: a techie or a politician? I'd choose the techie. But that's not the choice here. Who would you rather controlled your government: a techie or a politician? I'm afraid we're stuck with politics.

TECHNOCRACY VS. DEMOCRACY

There is an obvious response to the widening gap between technology and politics: let's find some people who can do both. Wouldn't it be better to be ruled by politicians who actually understand the technology they are trying to control? Shouldn't they have some expertise in those fields it is their job to regulate? If we can't have techies doing politics, let's at least have some politicians who can do tech.

This has been a regular lament of modern politics, especially as it has become more and more professionalised: where are the politicians who know about something other than politics? Professional politics has turned into a specialism with its own narrow skill set. Politicians are adept at particular tasks, such as winning elections, manipulating the newspapers, building coalitions, scheming against rivals, stabbing each other in the back: the Machiavellian tool kit, stripped of the grandeur of the Machiavellian worldview. Most current politicians treat politics as a career, and they start early, which gives them little opportunity to experience other ways of making a living. Yet almost everyone else makes their living in other ways. Politicians often seem to know very little about the world they are in the business of governing.

This problem is made worse by the increasing technical complexity of the world we now inhabit. Information technology is one example: we all use the internet, but how many of us understand how it actually works? We are entirely dependent on experts. So are the politicians. The same is true of finance, which has turned into a fiendishly complicated and arcane business. Plenty of bankers don't even understand the financial instruments they are trading, which have been dreamed up for them by math PhDs hidden away in back rooms out of view of their clients. The politicians are equally in the dark. Modern medicine is now highly specialised, making it very hard for individual doctors to keep up with the latest developments outside their own field. Many professionals often feel out of their depth without technical help. Why should politicians be any different?

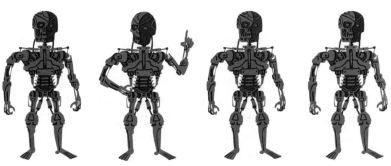

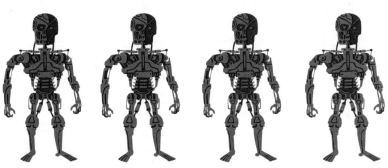

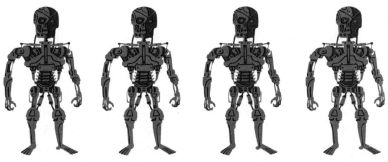

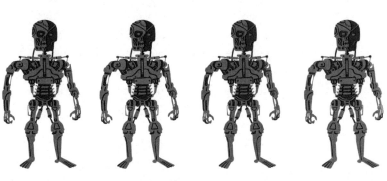

Faced with the premium on technical expertise, politics can look woefully out of touch. So the cry regularly goes up: bring in the experts! Let them help make the rules. The name for rule by experts is 'technocracy'. It sounds like a word from ancient Greece (*techne* meaning 'craft' and *kratos* meaning 'power'). In fact, it's an early twentieth-century invention, coined to describe the growing power of a new breed of industrial managers. The ancient Greeks did have a clear idea of expert rule, but it was not technocracy. The skill set they were looking for was expertise in politics, which was the summit of life. Ancient politics was meant to be an exercise in wisdom, something far above mere technical knowledge. It was a job for philosophers, not mechanics. *Techne* meant an understanding of how to make things work. Politics for the ancient Greeks was much more important than that: it was about how to live.

In the modern world, with its proliferation of scientific advances and its growing reliance on gadgets and gizmos, how we live is hopelessly dependent on someone understanding how to make things work. When we contemplate the worst that could happen, we don't usually envisage an outbreak of political un-wisdom. We think of technological breakdown: rogue machines, failed systems, corrupted networks, shuttered cashpoints, phones with no signal, planes that fall out of the sky. The people we rely on to prevent all this from happening needn't be especially wise; they just have to be clued up. The pull of modern technocracy comes in response to the fear that many professional politicians are clueless (and so are the people who elect them). Better to put the experts in charge, however deficient they may be in life knowledge or moral virtue. It's not as if the professional politicians are much good at those things either.

But experts in what? During the first half of the twentieth century, and particularly during the Great Depression, when politicians were doing their best to make a mess of everything, 'technocracy' meant rule by industrial engineers. Mass politics was assumed to be unsustainable without a steady supply of mass products: clothes, food, housing, communications, medicine, transport. The supply of these products depended on the control of complex and sophisticated systems. James Burnham, in his book *The Managerial Revolution* (1941), envisaged a future in which ultimate power lies not with the people who own the means of production (as Karl Marx thought) but with the people who manage it. Whether you had shares in a factory or worked in one, you were dependent on the experts who knew how to make a factory work. This knowledge was power. The politics of the future would belong to a class of bloodless technocrats who kept the industrial machinery working. Everyone else – elected politicians, financiers, trade unionists – would be answerable to them.

This was either an attractive vision or a horrific one, depending on your point of view. George Orwell's *1984* (written in 1948) was in part a miserably bleak satire of Burnham's technocratic society. Orwell thought Burnham had got it wrong: he had failed to account either for the vicious unpredictability of politics or for the restless creativity of the human spirit. But Burnham was wrong in another way as well. He overstated the power of industry. During the final third of the twentieth century, in parts of the West, finance staged a comeback as industrial production atrophied (and was usually franchised out to the developing world). The bankers took charge. Now, more important than owning a factory, or managing it, or working in it, was funding it. And more important than funding a factory was providing the funding for all sorts of other service enterprises that fuelled economic growth and fed consumer desires. Power came to reside with the people who managed the instruments of debt. It is to this class of people that we have come to look for technocratic solutions to our current political problems.

This is reflected in the rise to power of independent central bankers, who have been tasked with keeping a steady hand on the tiller of economic prosperity. Their job is to control inflation and smooth out the ups and downs of the economic cycle. Their independence is meant to protect them from the reach of interfering politicians, who are liable to screw these things up in response to the short-term demands of the electoral cycle. The Chairman of the US Federal Reserve these days has the sort of cachet and grandeur that a century ago belonged to the titans of industrial capitalism: the name Greenspan came to strike awe and fear as the name Rockefeller once did. When central bankers speak, or even when they don't say anything at all, markets tremble. When markets tremble, politicians quail. As James Carville, electoral adviser to Bill Clinton, once put it: 'I used to think if there was reincarnation, I wanted to come back as the president or the pope. Now I want to come back as the bond market. You can intimidate anybody.'

The changed composition of the new technocracy is shown by the people who get called in when the chips are down. At the height of the Euro crisis in 2011–12 two European countries – Italy and Greece – installed short-term 'technocratic' governments to break the political impasse. Unelected experts replaced elected politicians. And who were these experts? Most of them were bankers, financiers and economists. A sizeable number had worked either at or with one of the big US banks, notably Goldman Sachs. This included Mario Monti, the economist who became Italy's prime minister in 2011, and Lucas Papademos, the economist who became Greek prime minister in the same year. Technocracy has come to mean rule by those who understand the power of money.

But there is a puzzle about this sort of expertise: aren't the people brought in to solve the mess the same ones who got us into the mess in the first place? After all, the independent central bankers (and the teams of economists who work for them) failed in their primary task: they took their hands off the tiller and allowed the global economy to hit the rocks in 2008. The Euro crisis that blew up two years later was another failure of economic management. When politicians are forced to rely on the money men (and the occasional money woman) to sort out a crisis for which the money men were largely responsible, it looks less like technocracy and more like a protection racket: finance holding politics to ransom. These experts are in charge only because no one else knows the way out of the cave that they led us into.

The new technocracy sometimes appears to rely less on technical expertise than on networking skills. One thing the finance elite has that everyone else lacks is connections with each other. Working at Goldman Sachs doesn't guarantee that you know how to run the world; but it does guarantee that you know how to talk to other people who worked at Goldman Sachs in a language they will understand. Among the credentials of Monti and Papademos for crisis government was their good relationship with Mario Draghi, the chairman of the European Central Bank and another Goldman Sachs alumnus. High finance is an arcane business, which makes it important that the people who know its secrets can talk to each other. This isn't knowledge as power. It's obscurity as power.

The problem comes when the technocrats have to translate their rarefied talk back into a language that everyone else can understand. In politics, once you've made what you think is the right decision, you still have to convince other people of your right to make that decision. Being more knowledgeable than everyone else doesn't ensure political legitimacy, any more than being more violent does. Legitimacy is, as Weber said, a claim to power, and everything depends on whether people buy that claim. This is where technocrats tend to struggle. Their special knowledge is a hard sell, especially at election time.

Democratic technocrats are caught in a bind. Aloofness doesn't work. 'Trust me, I understand things you couldn't possibly understand' is a bad campaign slogan. But when technocrats try to pass themselves off as regular politicians it doesn't work either. 'Trust me, I'm not really an expert' is another very poor slogan. Monti discovered this when he campaigned for election in Italy in 2013. He sounded cold and detached when he talked economics. But he sounded empty and fake when he didn't. He struggled to present himself as a man of the people: he looked uncomfortable around children and animals, the stocks in trade of a political campaign. In the end he was trounced by the professional politicians. He was even trounced by Beppe Grillo, a comedian. That's why technocrats tend to avoid elections.

Along with soldiers, another profession Weber thought ill suited to politics was academics (a category that includes economists). The trouble is that academics are used to assuming that the best argument will win, and to supposing that they have the best argument. This makes them touchy and impatient when confronted with the mess and confusion of the real world. In politics there is no guarantee that the best argument will win. Nor is there any guarantee that other people will agree on what counts as the best argument. To succeed in politics requires a tolerance for uncertainty and an understanding of confusion. Above all, it requires a readiness to accept you can't win all the time, even when you think you are right. All politicians have to learn how to lose the argument and then come back for more. Weber thought that the best way to learn this was to do politics. Politics teaches you about failure.

That was why Weber, despite his occasional hankering for authoritarianism, had a strong preference for democracy. Fighting elections and then fighting in the legislature – or in the case of American presidents, fighting *with* the legislature – taught politicians that politics is a constant struggle, in which the essential thing is to keep going. Every political career must contain ups and downs, successes and rebuffs. The best politicians were the ones who had the stomach for the fight, learning from their mistakes without being destroyed by them, relishing their victories without being complacent about them. Academics rarely have these gifts. Bankers certainly don't. They are unused to failure, so that when it strikes they don't know how to handle it. The great thing about democracy is that no politician is too big to fail, which is why democratic states tend to survive.

A technocracy of economic experts is not the only model currently on show. High finance does not rule the roost everywhere. The Chinese political elite since 1989 has been dominated by engineers. The last three premiers – Jiang Zemin, Hu Jintao and Xi Jinping – all hold engineering degrees. Many other members of the Politburo trained as engineers, often at leading universities in the United States. In China industry, not finance, still sets the agenda. The Chinese banking sector is heavily regulated and subject to extensive political interference. The country's priority remains mass production. It is much closer to Burnham's

1978

REFORM IS CHINA'S SECOND REVOLUTION

DENG XIAOPING
REFORMIST

managerial society than anything we have in the West.

Of course, no one gets to the top of the Chinese Communist Party simply by being an engineer. These are all skilled and ruthless politicians, well versed in what it takes to outlast their rivals. None of them will be in any doubt that politics is a constant struggle. They have also had plenty of opportunity to learn from past failures. Present-day Chinese technocracy is a reaction against the catastrophic failures of the Mao years, above all the horrific famine of 1958–62, when ideological rigidity and dictatorial callousness cost the lives of 40 million people. The reformist Deng Xiaoping came to power in 1978 by defeating the loyalist faction known as the Whateverists – 'Q: What should we do? A: Whatever Mao would have wanted' – with the slogan 'Practice is the sole criterion for judging truth'. In contemporary Chinese politics, pragmatism has supplanted the cult of personality. This is the new Whateverism – 'Q: What should we do? A: Whatever works.'

However, the question that has yet to be answered is whether China's technocrats have the political skills to cope with all the lesser failures that are bound to accompany China's shift to a consumer economy and a world power. China is not a democracy. Its political elite fight with each other, but they don't have to fight elections in order to legitimise their power. That means they don't get regular lessons in losing the political argument. Weber thought democracy forced politicians to recognise the unavoidability of unintended consequences: in politics something will always come back to bite you. The danger for autocratic technocrats is that they treat politics as a machine they can control and regard every set-back as a technical problem they can correct. Instead of being forced to accept the messy unpredictability of political life, they use force to try to suppress it. The risk is that it can't be suppressed for ever. When the mess escapes their control, they have no resources to deal with it.

For now, China's technocrats remain in control. They have even managed to corral the internet as an instrument of managerial politics. The Chinese state employs tens of thousands of online snoopers, whose job is to oversee the way China's citizens use the new technology and make sure it doesn't get out of hand. This is not simply an exercise in censorship and suppression (though there is plenty of that).

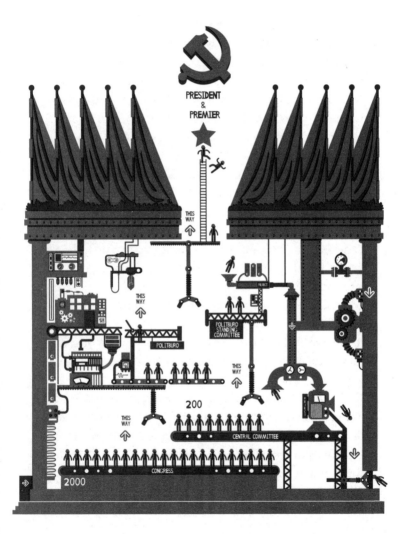

PRESIDENT
&
PREMIER

THIS
WAY

THIS
WAY

POLITBURO
STANDING
COMMITTEE

POLITBURO

THIS
WAY

200

THIS
WAY

CENTRAL COMMITTEE

CONGRESS

2000

It is also a way for the state to find out what irks its people, so as to head off those grievances before they become unmanageable. In the absence of elections, this is a valuable service. At the dawn of the information technology revolution in the 1990s there was a widespread hope that it spelt doom for authoritarians because they would not be able to control it. That is not what has happened. The internet has not democratised the Chinese state. Instead the Chinese state has used it to bypass democracy. Of course, it's not easy to control something as complex and multifarious as the web: it is a cumbersome and time-consuming business; it requires lots of money and lots of coercive power. That's why the only people who can do it are politicians.

Can they keep doing it? The information technology revolution is a long way from being over; in many respects it is only just beginning. At some point China's politicians will fail in their attempts to manage it: something will get away from them. Already China's citizens are proving adept at finding ways through and around the firewalls created by the Chinese state. They are also finding novel and subversive ways to voice their anger at the politicians, often using symbols and gestures the censors are too slow-witted to pick up on. Technology moves faster than politics. When technology escapes from political control, politicians face a choice: do they adapt to the change, or do they insist that it adapts to them? In a democracy politicians have no choice but to adapt. In an autocratic regime like contemporary China, however pragmatic and technically adept its rulers, there is always the temptation to double down on the use of force for fear of losing control altogether.

The Chinese Communist Party has learned from its past failures. Nonetheless, from its own perspective, it is still too big to fail. What happens when its determination to hold on to power collides with the unruliness of the modern information technology age remains to be seen. It is the great unknown of the twenty-first-century politics.

THE NEW ARISTOCRACY

Could the engineers make a political comeback in the West? Since 2008 it has been tough for financiers to assert their legitimacy as political decision-makers. Might the wizards of the tech industry have a better chance? There are signs that the disdain of Silicon Valley for the squalid world of politics is starting to dissipate. Tech giants who once thought they were above the miserable business of lawmaking have begun to take an interest in how laws get made. They've noticed that laws are going to get made anyway, so they might as well spend some of their vast resources trying to get the laws they want. This is not entirely self-interested. Many tech billionaires have begun to think about what all that money is for. They don't simply want to do no evil. They'd like to try to do some good. They are discovering that it's hard to do lasting good without political help.

However, there is little sign that the people who built the new technology are interested in actually doing politics themselves, rather than paying someone else to do it for them. They'll lobby; they'll fund; they'll campaign. Some of them will dabble with old-fashioned tools of political influence: Amazon founder Jeff Bezos has recently bought the venerable but impoverished *Washington Post*. But for now few have shown any interest in standing for office or offering their personal services to the government as agents of the state. It is nice to be able to influence Washington DC from Silicon Valley. But who wants to move from Silicon Valley to lead the relentless and poorly rewarded Washington life? The moves go the other way. In Britain, no one works for David Cameron who used to work for Google. But a number of people have gone to work for Google who used to work for David Cameron.

This isn't just a story about tech. Many people retain an interest in politics – we all would like laws made to suit us – but fewer and fewer people seem interested in being politicians. It's simply not a very attractive job. In a world of myriad possibilities, especially for those who have the technical abilities that bring lavish rewards in the private sector, politics looks like a real grind. Politicians have to work very hard, under intense scrutiny, for little reward. They sometimes suffer public contempt and media abuse; more often their hard work is greeted with indifference. Their lives are scrutinised for evidence of personal moral failings that can be used as a stick to beat them with. Their families and friends occasionally get dragged into a crucible of media cynicism and censoriousness that engulfs them all. True, successful politicians get to exercise real power now and then, which must be a thrill. But most politicians are not successful: they labour away, scrabbling for votes, striving for influence, only to find that someone has beaten them to it. While politicians are busy doing politics, the power to make a real difference often seems to pass them by.

The result is that contemporary politics doesn't just require a particular skill set. It also demands an appetite for that gruelling way of life. I don't have it. Do you? The class of people interested in doing politics is shrinking. This is good news if you do happen to have an appetite for it. The competition is not what it was, so that a desire to get into politics is often all it takes to be given that chance. In Britain the current crop of leading politicians is drawn from a remarkably narrow set of political careerists, most of whom have been doing politics since they were at university. Many of them were at university together.

The present British prime minister, foreign secretary, chancellor of the exchequer, education secretary, leader of the opposition, shadow chancellor and shadow home secretary were all part of the same generation of Oxford politics students. I didn't go to Oxford, but I did go to the same school as David Cameron – Eton – at the same time he did. When we were there, he was pointed out to me as someone who wanted to be prime minister. We were sixteen. Eton is an absurdly privileged school full of well-connected and ambitious boys, but few had an interest in politics: most wanted to be bankers or film stars. I only heard of one other who wanted to be prime minister. His name was Boris Johnson. Watching these two rise effortlessly to the top of British politics makes it hard to believe that the greasy pole is as greasy as it used to be.

Eton and Oxford: it sounds more like a reversion to aristocracy than a form of technocracy. In France there has long been a tradition of grooming leading politicians and bureaucrats from within a narrowly selective educational system. Many of those who reach the top of French public life have known each other ever since they were students together at the École Normale Supérieure. Nonetheless, the French version is avowedly technocratic, in a classical as well as a modern sense. The aim is to promote academic excellence geared towards high-minded public service, even if the invariable result is to produce a cosy club of well-connected individuals. The system dates back to the end of the eighteenth century (the ENS was founded in 1793), when the ideals of the revolution demanded a new breed of enlightened administrators. These people were meant to be selected on merit to replace the traditional aristocracy. The current British version looks more like a throwback to an earlier eighteenth-century form of politics, when merit mattered less than privilege and family ties. British politics is in the hands of a narrow elite who happen to share the right background. Where you start out matters more than where you want to end up.

However, this is not simply a Tory phenomenon. The leadership of the Labour party is also made up of individuals who are connected to each other by ties of family and education. Labour politics has been dominated in recent years by the rivalry between two brothers – David and Ed Miliband – who were both brought up doing politics by their Marxist academic father, Ralph Miliband. The Marxism didn't stick, but the connection with the world of politics did (both boys were mingling with the high-ups in the Labour Party from their teenage years). In future, Labour politics may be dominated by another family: the husband and wife team of Ed Balls and Yvette Cooper, currently Ed Miliband's nearest rivals (now that his brother has gone off to New York in a sulk). Nor is this simply a British phenomenon. Family ties play an increasingly prominent role in American politics. The next presidential election could be between the two clans who continue to dominate American political life: Hillary Clinton vs. Jeb Bush, the wife of one president vs. the son and brother of two more. People are already speculating about some future contest between Chelsea Clinton, daughter of Hillary, and George P. Bush, son of Jeb. At the state level, many families have a strong hold on the top jobs, from the Cuomos in New York (the current governor is the son of a former governor) to the Browns in California (ditto). The children of politicians are as likely to become politicians as they have ever been.

The new aristocracy is not just made up of the traditional propertied elites using politics to preserve their own wealth and status. This is a phenomenon that cuts across party lines and ideological divisions: political families don't necessarily defend the rights of the privileged few. (The most aristocratic of all, the Kennedys, were also among the most progressive.) The narrowing of the political class through family ties is a function of the professionalisation of politics and the increasingly high barriers to entry. Politics has become a specialised business, and the best way to get good at it is to do a lot of it. It helps to start early. It also helps to have connections with anyone who can give you a head start. At the same time, politics has become a widely despised profession. (A recent survey suggested that most American parents would rather their children did almost anything else.) So it helps to have parents or siblings who can encourage you to give it a go, notwithstanding what the rest of the world thinks. Politics is hardly unique in this respect. Lots of children end up doing what their parents did, simply for reasons of familiarity. My father is an academic sociologist, and here I am writing this book. I don't really know why it turned out like that. I don't think it's especially sinister, though it's not very imaginative on my part. I suspect that for many politicians the situation is not much different.

Does it matter that the political class is shrinking? In one sense, no. It is a sign of broad satisfaction with the political system that most people don't want to have anything to do with politics if they can help it. If they were really unhappy, the high entry barriers would not put them off. More likely in their rage they would tear them down. There are far greater incentives to get involved in politics when things are going badly than when they are going well. That was one of Hobbes's fundamental insights. Politics in Syria is awful, which is why many Syrians want more involvement, to stop the Assads from running the show for their own benefit. The Assads aren't in charge because they happen to be a family with an interest in politics; they are thugs and tyrants who have despoiled the state for their own advantage. The only way to stop them is to take politics away from them. Denmark is a country whose current leader is also a member of a political dynasty: the prime minister, Helle Thorning-Schmidt, is married to Stephen Kinnock, the son of the former British Labour leader Neil Kinnock and his wife, Glenys, a one-time MEP and ex-minister for Europe.

This cosiness irritates plenty of Danes, especially when it emerged that Stephen Kinnock, who works for the World Economic Forum, had been avoiding paying income tax in Denmark. However, it didn't annoy ordinary Danes enough to make them want to become politicians; they just wanted Kinnock to pay more tax. The new political aristocracy riles voters when they can be bothered to think about it, and occasionally it scandalises them. But it doesn't politicise them. That's the basic reason it exists in the first place.

However, there are real dangers to this narrowing of the political class. It opens up a gap between politicians and the rest of us, which can breed contempt both ways. If we think that professional politics is only for people who happen to have a peculiar interest in politics, we will start to look down on them as weirdos. Meanwhile, the politicians will start to look down on us as fools, because we don't understand the business they are in. The disdain many voters feel for professional politicians is matched by the disdain many professional politicians feel for the voters. Each thinks the other lot don't get it. As the gap grows, it becomes easier for politicians to gravitate towards their fellow elites, who at least have a respect for insider knowledge. The political network interlocks with networks of financial, technological and military expertise, which locks the public out. A narrow class of politicians is bound to have a skewed view of the world it inhabits, because its members rarely get to see how their world looks from the outside. The failure of the political elite to anticipate the financial crisis of 2008 is evidence of how easily closed-off groups can lose sight of what they are doing. Aristocracies, old and new, always have massive blind spots.

Ordinary citizens haven't given up on politics entirely. In some respects there has been a proliferation of political activity beyond the traditional outlets. As the membership of mainstream political parties has fallen away and voter turnout has declined across the Western world, irregular political campaigning has expanded. Concerned individuals often coalesce around issues that reflect their own particular interests. The new information technology has been an enormous help in this regard, enabling ad hoc pressure groups to form and allowing like-minded individuals to find each other and share their concerns. But this too creates an imbalance between the political class and the rest. Professional politics is becoming more concentrated at the same time that citizen politics is becoming more fragmented. The new technology brings people together, but it also separates them out by hiving them off into online silos of political concern. The connections that are made through the new technology can be speedy, but for that reason they may also be superficial. Malcolm Gladwell wrote in 2010 that 'the revolution will not be tweeted'. He is probably right. Politics change requires more lasting and durable connections. There is a danger that a proliferation of unconventional political campaigns leaves the political class to sew up the lasting connections among themselves.

Above all, there is the danger that Benjamin Constant warned against. If we leave routine politics in the hands of a narrow group of specialists, we won't know how to take it back from them when we need it. The multiple scandals of the last few years – the banking scandal, the MPs' expenses scandal, the phone-hacking scandal, the GCHQ/NSA scandal – have tended to generate a widespread sense of powerlessness alongside the occasional spasms of fury. The political elite have been exploiting our inattention to shore up their own position. We would like to hold them to account for their temerity, but we lack the tools to do it: their superior knowledge of how politics works leaves us feeling impotent. People who think they can pick up politics when they need it often find that when they really need it they don't know where to find it. The professionals run rings round them. The only way to learn how to do politics is to keep on doing it, in good times as well as bad. We need more politics and we need more politicians.

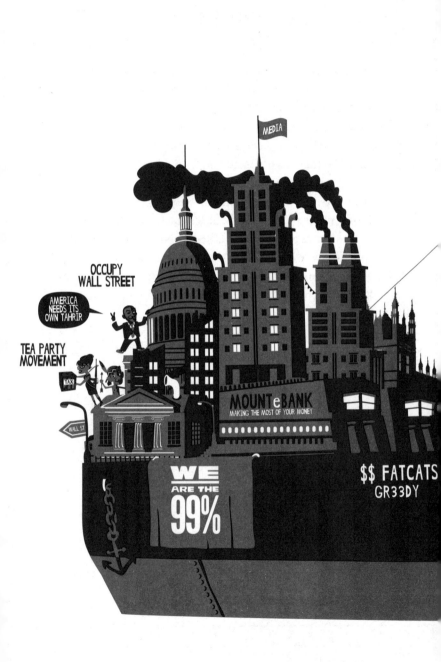

3
JUSTICE

AS BAD AS IT GETS

Present-day Syria, as bad as it is, is not the most afflicted place in the world. For a long time that title possibly belonged to the Democratic Republic of the Congo (DRC). A civil war has been raging there on and off for nearly two decades (currently more off than on). The Syrian civil war has confounded the international community, which has not known what to do to stop it. But at least it has been thinking about it; occasionally it has been thinking about little else. The war in the DRC rarely got international attention, and almost no one was thinking about how to stop it. Few people outside the country were thinking about it at all. Like Syria, the DRC is a past victim of imperial exploitation. But nothing that happened in Syria can compare to the horrors inflicted on the Belgian Congo at the end of the nineteenth century. The country was pillaged for its rich supply of natural resources (above all, rubber), and its native population was brutally worked to extract the wealth for their imperial masters. Many millions died as a result. The Congolese have been the victims of genocide and persistent exploitation. The country remains impoverished and divided. Life expectancy is currently around forty-five, not very much higher than it was in England in Hobbes's time. Per capita GDP is $300 per year. This is more than ten times lower than Syria. It is more than one hundred times lower than Denmark.

These aren't God-given facts. They don't reflect racial differences. This is a man-made catastrophe. We did it. So why don't we do more to fix it? The people of Europe, only a few thousand miles to the north, lead lives that are entirely remote from those experienced by the inhabitants of central Africa. This is one reason why they don't do anything about the gulf between them: it doesn't impinge. But that is no justification for doing nothing. The gulf is real, and it is grotesque. It raises an obvious question: how can it possibly be fair? Why should one group of people, simply because of an accident of birth, have the chance to lead comfortable and secure lives while others have little chance, through no fault of their own? The population of the DRC is close to 80 million, roughly the same as the population of Germany. The number of people in Africa who live on less than $1.25 (or 1 Euro) a day is nearly equivalent to the total population of Western Europe. One planet: two worlds.

Of course, it would be a mistake to paint the DRC as nothing but horror. The West of the country is much more stable than the East. Congolese society contains pockets of prosperity, just as prosperous societies contain pockets of misery. Moreover, happiness is not just a material concept. Even the very poorest people can experience it: it's horribly patronising to assume otherwise. Nor are the grimmest parts of the DRC representative of much of the rest of Africa, where relative political stability, alongside the resources freed up by the new technology, is spurring economic growth and dragging millions of people out of the worst sort of poverty (as many as 100 million in the last ten years alone). Nevertheless, the widespread poverty that persists is an enduring calamity. Having to scrape an existence on less than a Euro a day is no way to live. The miserable burden often falls on women, whose lives are blighted by extreme poverty in countless different ways, ranging from the absence of educational opportunities to the lack of basic healthcare to the persistent threat of violence. Anyone from the developed world would find it an intolerable existence. So why do we tolerate it for others?

Politics can make the difference between heaven and hell on earth. But politics seems remarkably indifferent to closing the gap between them. Previous chapters were about the importance of politics and its scope. This chapter is about its limits. Where we most need politics to help – where the need for help is most obvious – is often where politics fails to deliver.

Calling the recent plight of the DRC a civil war can make it sound more organised than it really is. Some areas of the country have effectively been reduced to a condition of anarchy, not far off a Hobbesian state of nature. The same is true of its smaller northern neighbour the Central African Republic, which has been described by its own prime minister as 'an anarchy, a non-state'. There is no order and no security: armed gangs rule, the basic institutions of civil society have ceased to function, life is precarious and horribly unpredictable. In a civil war people are afraid of the other side winning. In parts of central Africa it can be hard to know how anyone could win. In these circumstances, it makes sense to be afraid of everyone. But if this is the Hobbesian nightmare, Hobbes is little help in showing how to get out of it. That's because his thought experiment wasn't designed for people in a state of nature. It was designed for people who have a functioning politics to warn them not to dabble with the alternatives. Hobbes explains *why* we need to escape the state of nature. He doesn't explain *how* to escape if you're stuck there.

The answer may seem obvious: these countries require a functioning state. They need to choose politics. But which politics? There are by now lots of alternatives to choose from. The best would probably be something like Denmark. But it seems absurd to say the DRC should strive to be more like Denmark, given the vast gulf that separates them. The stability of Danish politics is a product of Denmark's own particular history and geography, and it has multiple inter-locking causes: the Protestant Reformation and the spread of literacy; the rise of organised farming and labour move-ments in the nineteenth century; the end of military con-flict and the stabilisation of Scandinavian borders; the free exchange of ideas and goods with the rest of Europe. You can hardly take this package and transplant it to twenty-first-century Africa. But nor is it clear that you can cherry-pick bits of it to see if they can work their magic independently. Yes, the DRC could do with organised farmers and labour movements, peaceful relations with its neighbours, greater access to international trade. But how do you achieve these things in isolation from each other? How do you get to be Denmark without being Denmark?

Denmark is far from the only model available. There are plenty of other political options between chaos and peaceful security. The world is full of countries that are better off in political terms than the DRC but worse off than Denmark. There are authoritarian technocracies like China (on the largest scale) and Singapore (on the smallest), populist democracies like Venezuela, semi-constitutional theocra-cies like Iran, semi-militarised democracies like Sri Lanka and semi-democratic oligarchies like Russia. Political scien-tists call these 'hybrid' regimes: they are a mish-mash of dif-ferent elements, often combining bits of democratic prac-tice with elements of authoritarianism. All of these regime types have plenty of things wrong with them, including varying levels of corruption and abuse of power by their rulers. But they all have functioning states and a degree of political stability. So did Syria until very recently. At present its politics has broken down, but just a few years ago it was a relatively stable regime, if a very unpleasant one: a repressive one-party state. Should the DRC at least try to become more like pre-war Syria, which worked in part, before it thinks about becoming Denmark, which works in full? Again, the proposition seems absurd. No one should wish the politics of Syria on any other nation. Nor would it be any easier to make the transition. Syrian politics is a product of its own particular history and geography. You can't get to Denmark via Syria.

Hobbes thought it was a bad idea to compare regime types because it breeds resentment and wishful thinking. People will want something better than what they've got, imagining that the grass is always greener. Yet once there is clear evidence that some regime types do work better than others, it is very hard not to compare and, if you are in one of the ones that doesn't work, wish for something better. What happens if the grass really is greener? When we are able to see the difference successful states can make, it is reasonable to want to know how they did it. The problem is knowing what to do with that knowledge. Seeing how they did it doesn't tell you how to do it yourself.

This puzzle was apparent within a century of Hobbes writing *Leviathan*. The founding father of modern comparative politics was a French aristocrat, Charles-Louis de Secondat, Baron de Montesquieu, whose great work *The Spirit of the Laws* was published in 1748. By this point Hobbes's argument about Lucca being no better than Constantinople seemed very out of date. It had been overtaken by events. Now there was something that clearly worked better than either: the revised British constitution, which had emerged from the revolution of 1688. Under this system power was divided between king and parliament, and between the two houses of parliament – Lords and Commons – allowing each to act as a check on the other. This was much preferable to any political system that concentrated power in the hands of a single ruler. Montesquieu certainly preferred it. 'In Turkey,' he wrote, 'where these powers are united in the Sultan's person, the subjects groan under the most dreadful oppression.' Italian city-states were just as unsatisfactory. Their constitutions concentrated power in the hands of their republican rulers, so that 'the government is obliged to have recourse to as violent methods for its support as even that of the Turks.' No one benefits from a regime of violence and fear. Stable politics requires restraint. A constitution on the British model could provide it.

However, Britain could not serve as a reliable model for other places wanting to know how to acquire such a constitution. There were two reasons for this. First, every country's political system was a product of its particular circumstances. Montesquieu was adamant that geography, history, climate, culture and custom all went together to make up a nation's politics. The British constitution did not emerge ready-made out of the revolution of 1688. It was also a result of the long history that preceded the revolution, and it drew on all sorts of influences, from ancient republicanism through medieval folklore to memories of the civil war, twisted and adapted to suit the needs of the modern age. A country's constitution was not simply a legal arrangement. It was more like a physiological condition: the thing that makes the body politic tick. Each country had its own. They might superficially resemble each other – various northern European countries in Montesquieu's time had features in common with England – but they all had their own individual character. Because these constitutions do not emerge out of thin air, they can never be transplanted ready-made to somewhere else.

Second, Britain's constitution worked because it was complex. What Montesquieu called 'constitutional monarchy' was preferable to more straightforward systems, whether straight monarchy or straight democracy. These suffered from the disadvantage of their simplicity: when something went wrong, there was nothing to stop everything from running out of control. Under a constitution like the British one the

THIS CONSTITUTION CAN NEVER BE TRANSPLANTED TO SOMEWHERE ELSE

INSTRUCTIONS
FRANCE

MONTESQUIEU

116

different parts of the political system restrained each other, moderating excesses and limiting expectations. The interplay was the essence of the system. So although the difference between a good constitution and a bad one was easy to summarise – just as a healthy person is easy to tell apart from a sick one – a good constitution could never in itself be easily summarised. Indeed, if you could sum it up in a few sentences, it almost certainly wouldn't work. The American constitution, which was influenced by some of Montesquieu's ideas, is sometimes assumed to be a simple document, because it is relatively short by modern standards. But it is far from simple. If it were, it could hardly have lasted so long. Americans have spent more than two hundred years mining its depths, and they are nowhere near finished.

As the US example shows, we have come a long way from the eighteenth-century British version of constitutional monarchy (which was effectively the system the American revolutionaries rejected, though the influence of Montesquieu shows they were pretty conflicted about it). In different places and at different times, countries have democratised their constitutions without relapsing into crude and fearful politics. Elected heads of state have replaced kings and queens (except in places like Britain and its former dependencies, or the Scandinavian countries, where kings and queens have simply been deprived of all their powers). The franchise has gradually been extended to include those categories of adults who were previously excluded (in Montesquieu's time the British electorate constituted just 2 per cent of the total population, all of them propertied, Anglican men). British Catholics, Jews and working men were enfranchised during the course of the nineteenth century. Women did not get the vote until the second decade of the twentieth century, and not on the same terms as men until 1928. The voting age was lowered from twenty-one to eighteen in 1969. Now there is talk of lowering it to sixteen. The European Court of Human Rights has recently ruled to extend the franchise to serving prisoners, though the current British government is resisting.

Other countries have followed a similar pattern of slow and choppy progress towards greater democracy, some considerably slower and choppier than others. (French women did not get the vote until 1945, more than 150 years after the men; in Switzerland women did not get the vote until 1971; the country that moved to universal suffrage for men and women earliest was New Zealand, in 1893.) Elsewhere the change has often been quicker. Many countries have democratised rapidly, some, such as Japan, in the aftermath of the Second World War and others, such as Poland, following the end of the Cold War. Modern democratic citizens have now acquired an extensive portfolio of rights backed up by increasingly elaborate systems of law. Discrimination on the grounds of gender, sexual orientation, race or religion, though it has hardly been abolished, has been greatly curtailed. The direction of change is not all one way. In the United States the Supreme Court recently ruled invalid key parts of the Voting Rights Act of 1965, paving the way for renewed discretion on the part of individual states to disenfranchise individual voters. Democratic progress can never be taken for granted. Nevertheless, the evolution and the spread of the politics of constitutional restraint since Montesquieu wrote have been remarkable.

Yet in one respect the situation remains unchanged. In their best-selling 2012 book *Why Nations Fail* the political economists Daron Acemoglu and James Robinson set out to explain the fundamental difference between good and bad politics. Their explanation is very simple (or, as they call it, 'parsimonious'). Politics works when it is 'inclusive': i.e., when people with power still have good reasons to take account of what others want. Politics does not work when it is 'extractive': i.e., when people with power see it as an opportunity to take what they can get while they have the chance. (In the jargon of political science this is called 'rent-seeking', meaning that political office is treated as a means of extracting rent.) In inclusive states, rival groups realise that

they are better off taking turns to pursue their goals, because the alternative of pursuing them regardless would be worse for everyone. Under extractive regimes, rival groups do not think it is worth waiting. Politics becomes now or never. So extractive politics is essentially a failure of trust: a politics of 'diffidence', as Hobbes would call it, leading to endless pre-emptive strikes. The key to achieving lasting stability and prosperity is to move from an extractive regime to an inclusive one. On this account, Britain's constitutional revolution in 1688 remains a pivotal moment in modern history. Every state, if it is to be successful, needs something similar.

Acemoglu and Robinson insist that there is nothing deterministic about their account of political success. Their aim is to show that the plight of impoverished nations is not predetermined by climate, or geography, or culture, or religion. No nation is fated to fail. They point to the case of North and South Korea: essentially the same country, with the same geography, made up of the same people. But the divergent political paths the two states have followed since 1953 has made one among the wealthiest nations in the world and the other among the poorest. The difference inclusive politics makes could hardly be starker.

But though it is easy to summarise what makes the difference, it is very hard to know how to make it happen. The problem is that the move to inclusive political institutions is always highly contingent: it is a consequence of the complicated interplay between chance historical events and deep-rooted social forces. It is impossible to stage-manage. You can't 'do' 1688–89 anywhere except in Britain in 1688–89, and even then the leading actors were hardly in control of what they were doing. It was a complex, haphazard, fractious process. Stable political outcomes are too dependent on conditional political choices to be readily translatable from one setting to another. Context trumps everything. The crucial feature of inclusivity is that it is *internal* to the state in question: the various actors come to see their choices as framed by the choices of other members of the state.

Attempting to impose inclusivity on states from the outside won't work. It would mean treating inclusive politics as though it were extractive: i.e., as an outcome you can force on people. Extractive politics, by contrast, can be imposed from the outside, because it is by definition a kind of imposition. Bad politics translates from one place to another much more readily than good politics. It only requires ruthlessness. Tolstoy says at the beginning of *Anna Karenina* that all happy families are alike, whereas every unhappy family is unhappy in its own particular way. In politics it's the other way round. Unhappy states are relatively alike: they are all places where the same sorts of exploitative behaviour recur. Happy states have to learn how to be happy in their own particular way.

There is another big difficulty with thinking that

inclusivity is the solution to the problem of political failure. Inclusive states are also extractive. They take advantage of their relative stability and prosperity to exploit nations less fortunate than themselves. States exist in competition with other states and often ensnare them in lasting relations of exploitation and domination. Parsimonious theories of politics tend to ignore this. (It is one of the gaps in Hobbes's account that he neglects the role of economic competition between states, preferring to think of stable states as economically self-sufficient.) The 1688 revolution in Britain set this country on the path to

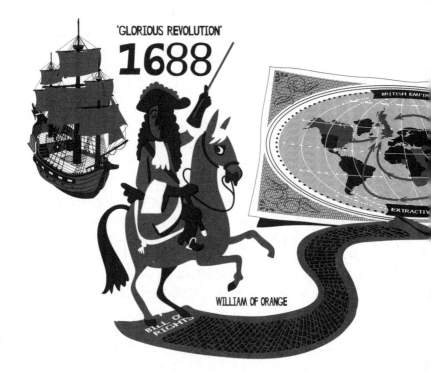

'GLORIOUS REVOLUTION'
1688

BRITISH EMPIRE

EXTRACTIVE

WILLIAM OF ORANGE

BILL OF RIGHTS

democracy, but it also set many other countries around the world on the path to domination by Britain. The move by Britain towards stable parliamentary government before anyone else produced, among other things, the British Empire, which was a highly extractive regime, whatever its current defenders may say. The British did not take turns with their colonies.

The hideous treatment of the Congo in the late nineteenth century – one of the worst examples of extractive politics in all history – was also undertaken by an inclusive state. Late nineteenth-century Belgium was a constitutional monarchy which, despite being riven by deep social, cultural and ethnic divisions (workers vs. capitalists, Catholics vs. liberals, Flemings vs. Walloons), had found a way to hold itself together. This relative political stability enabled its rulers to build themselves an empire: tiny Belgium got to plunder the heart of Africa. The ability to build an empire enabled Belgium's rulers to offset some of the risks of domestic political instability. It was a poisonous compact. Acemoglu and Robinson are right to say that nothing in politics is inevitable: bad political outcomes are no more predetermined than good ones. Inclusive states don't have to export violence and exploitation. However, the historical record shows that they often do.

Inclusivity is no sort of political panacea. It is hard to achieve. It is hard to translate. Sometimes it is hard even

BRITISH CONSTITUTION

PARLIAMENT, USING THE
POWER OF THE CROWN, ENACTS
LAW WHICH NO OTHER BODY
CAN CHALLENGE

to identify. Though the difference between inclusive and extractive states is often clear (South vs. North Korea), it can be very difficult to know where to classify individual states (just as it can be hard to say whether an individual person is healthy or not). Which, for instance, is contemporary South Africa? Apartheid South Africa was self-evidently an extractive regime. But since 1991 South Africa has mixed constitutional reform with continuing economic exclusion. For an ostensibly inclusive state the country has yet to extend the advantages of its political transformation to large numbers of its citizens, who remain very disadvantaged. Poor, black South Africans are both better off than they have ever been and no better off than they have ever been. By contrast, the present Chinese state is essentially an extractive regime – the Chinese Communist Party does not take it in turns to rule and is plagued with corruption as a result – yet its rulers have tried to include as many Chinese as possible in the benefits of the country's growing prosperity. China is currently investing heavily in Africa, including in the DRC, which has seen significant improvements to parts of its infrastructure. (China is certainly putting much more money into the rest of Africa than the South African government is.) At the same time China is extracting large amounts of Africa's natural resources for its own domestic use. The Chinese are playing a double game in Africa. It will take a long time to know who the winners and the losers are.

There is nothing straightforward about political success and political failure, however stark the difference between them. Getting politics right remains a fearsomely difficult business.

NOT THE END OF HISTORY

However, at some moments in history this gets quickly forgotten. One such moment occurred in 1989. The end of the Cold War was so sudden and so welcome that it was tempting to read it as a morality tale. Democracy had won. Communism had lost, confirming the final defeat of totalitarianism over the course of the twentieth century. The difference between good politics and bad politics looked glaringly obvious. History seemed to have given its answer to the problem of politics. The answer was Western liberal democracy.

The person who often gets blamed for pushing this simplistic view is Francis Fukuyama, thanks to an article he published in the summer of 1989 (a few months before the Berlin Wall came down), which he called 'The End of History'. Blaming Fukuyama for over-egging the events of 1989 is not really fair. He did not argue that history was coming to an end in that year. His article merely claimed that over the course of modern political history the advantages of liberal democracy had become increasingly apparent, to the point that it was hard to come up with any viable alternatives. It didn't follow that democracy was about to triumph everywhere, or that the existing democracies were going to have it all their own way. Fukuyama thought plenty could still go wrong. He was worried that, without plausible alternatives, Western democracy was liable to become stale and unimaginative. Just as Hobbes has an undeserved reputation as a pessimist, Fukuyama has an undeserved reputation as an optimist. He felt the coming ascendancy of democracy ought to be approached with considerable trepidation.

Fukuyama was right to be worried. But he was worrying about the wrong thing. Victory in the Cold War did not leave Western democracy flat and lifeless. It made it reckless and cavalier. The democracies went wrong because they got carried away with their success. They mistook it for a positive achievement. It wasn't. The triumph of democracy during the twentieth century had essentially been a negative one. Democracy didn't come out on top because of all the good it did, but rather because of all the bad it avoided. Churchill was speaking the truth when in 1947 he called democracy 'the worst system of government apart from all the others that have been tried from time to time'.

Modern democracy remains at root a politics of restraint. It is a good way to stop the worst from happening. This can make an enormous practical difference. As the Indian economist Amartya Sen has shown, democracies do not suffer from famines, because the potential victims can let their governments know what is happening in time to prevent it. The historical record indicates that democracies do not go to war with each other. Democracies allow individual citizens the opportunity to register discontent with their politicians. Fukuyama thought the recognition of personal dissatisfaction was a key reason for the general satisfaction with democracy, because it confers dignity on the individual citizen. Democracy lets people let off steam, which stops them boiling over. Nonetheless, these remain negative achievements. They are not sufficient to count as an answer to the problems of politics.

What has happened since Fukuyama proclaimed the end of history shows that the politics of restraint cannot do everything. Big mistakes are made when we assume it can. Democracy has not, for instance, solved the problem of inequality. Since the mid-1970s, and more rapidly since the end of the Cold War, the Western world has seen inequality widen. This has been most noticeable in the United States. The rich have got much richer over recent decades. Economic gains have been largely confined to the wealthiest 1 per cent of the population, and even within that group it is those at the very top who have seen the biggest advances in their net worth. The richest 0.01 per cent, or just 16,000 households, now own nearly 5 per cent of America's total wealth (for an average of $23,000,000 each), a proportion of the spoils not seen for more than a century, since the last age of the robber barons. At the same time the poor are not much better off than they were a generation ago. Many of the middle classes are significantly worse off. Wages have stagnated while investment income has boomed.

It looks like a politically toxic combination: to those who have shall be given more, while to those who are struggling shall be given nothing at all. Why do the not-so-rich put up with it? Why don't they use the political system to redress the balance? After all, the 99 per cent could easily outvote the 1 per cent. The US is meant to be a democracy. But American democracy was not designed to allow large-scale redistributions of income at the behest of the voters. If anything, it was designed to prevent it. The founders of the American republic were worried that the democratic majority might use its power to take money from the wealthy minority. (Their most acute fear was that the poor would vote for a cancellation of all debts.) So they organised a complicated political system intended to make it difficult for the majority to get its way, or even to know what its way is. The politics of restraint stops politicians from taking things that don't belong to them. It protects people from the abuse of political power. It doesn't empower politics to protect them from economic injustice.

The result is that liberal democracies can allow large structural inequalities to build up over time. Modern democratic citizens have plenty of ways to complain about politics, but they often lack the resources to turn their personal dissatisfactions into collective action. It usually takes a disaster to trigger structural change. The United States only moved to a welfare system that could provide for its poorest citizens after the Great Depression, which threatened the country with collapse. Europe only moved to its relatively egalitarian welfare states following the calamity of the Second World War. Without a disaster, liberal democracies have a tendency to drift towards unfairness. Citizens who are protected from political concentrations of power are left exposed to economic concentrations of power. This is what happened in an accelerated fashion after 1989. The absence of any serious threats to democracy allowed the democracies to slide into a new gilded age.

What can we do about this? One option, though not a very attractive one, is to hope for a fresh disaster to shake up the system. The crash of 2008 was bad, but so far not bad enough to bring about structural change. (In 2013 the megarich are relatively even better off than they were in 2007.) So we would need something worse. Something worse than 2008 would have to be very bad indeed. Who wants another global depression or a world war? Nothing seems worth that. We need to consider alternative remedies.

Since the 1970s, two possible answers to the problem of inequality have presented themselves. The first comes from political philosophy. In recent decades philosophers have devoted extraordinary amounts of time and energy to thinking up schemes of justice that might be consistent with liberal democracy but able to plug its gaping holes of unfairness. The best-known of these schemes is the one associated with the philosopher John Rawls, who argued that in a democracy everyone should be able to recognise the essential fairness of a broadly redistributive economic system – one that works, as he put it, to the advantage of the least advantaged. Rawls constructed a thought experiment to make his case. Imagine if you didn't know if you were rich or poor. What political system would you want? Rawls thought we would all choose to insure against being very poor, even if it cost us the chance to be very rich. The point of this thought experiment was to get people to think about democratic justice in impersonal terms. The problem is that it was only a thought experiment. Actually existing democracies encourage people to think about justice in highly personal terms: personal abuses, personal complaints, personal remedies. That's why it can be so hard to get even the most disadvantaged citizens to see their predicament in the round.

Rawls published his best-known book, *A Theory of Justice*, in 1971. It has dominated American political philosophy ever since. Yet over the same period American democracy has moved in the opposite direction to the one he proposed. When Rawls died in 2002, some of the tributes noted that his ideas were finally being picked up in the speeches and writings of an American president. Unfortunately that president was not George W. Bush, who was then in the White House. It was Josiah Bartlet, the Nobel-prize-winning economist and all-round good guy who occupied the make-believe White House in *The West Wing*. Rawls's ideas are powerful philosophy. The danger is that they turn into fantasy politics.

More recently a different philosophical approach to the problem of structural injustice has emerged. If modern democracy results in a thin and essentially negative conception of politics, why not try to beef it up by reconnecting it with its republican roots? The core idea of classical republicanism is that people need *power*, not just protection. They require this power to resist the power of the rich to exploit their material advantages to dominate public life. A neutral politics of fairness is not enough to remedy the imbalance. Republican justice requires an active politics of redress. The inspiration for this idea is often Machiavelli, who has been resuscitated by contemporary political philosophers in an attempt to break free from the long shadow of Hobbes.

Although Machiavelli is essentially a pre-modern thinker, his version of republicanism has all sorts of possible modern uses. It can apply wherever one group is dominated by another: the poor by the rich, women by men, children by adults, patients by doctors, even animals by humans. The ideal of non-domination implies that politics has to provide a meaningful corrective for every such relationship: it needs to give anyone who is on the receiving end of unequal treatment the means to fight back. These tools will inevitably go beyond conventional political rights, such as the right to vote. That is never going to be enough on its own. (Certainly it won't work for animals.) Non-domination requires material help. The disadvantaged need ready access to information, communication, education and representation. This means prioritising social institutions such as trade unions and welfare schemes like universal healthcare and free childcare. It also takes money. If every adult was paid a living wage by the state, no woman need find herself economically trapped in an abusive relationship. She could always afford to get out. That's not the republicanism Machiavelli had in mind, but it's a plausible extension of his confrontational view of politics.

Contemporary republican philosophers don't want to go back to seventeenth-century Lucca: there wasn't much healthcare there, universal or otherwise. Rather, they want to build on modern democracy to enable it to reach its full potential. Non-domination is a negative idea, but it's a much richer negative idea than the rival liberal democratic idea of being left alone. Yet, precisely because we have got so used to being left alone, republicanism is a hard sell in modern democracies. It makes heavy political demands on us and places a high premium on full political participation (a far higher premium than Constant did, and even he was asking for a lot). It is a more robust political philosophy than Rawls's, because it takes power seriously. Nonetheless it does not fit neatly with liberal democracy, no matter how well the two can be made to complement each other on paper. Tackling structural inequality often goes against the grain of the politics of restraint.

That is the lesson of the other possible remedy for rising inequality: democratic populism. The countries that have made the biggest strides in reducing the gap between the very rich and the very poor have also ridden roughshod over many liberal democratic safeguards. Venezuela under Hugo Chávez had, on his death in 2012, the lowest measure for inequality anywhere in Latin America. At the same time, his years in power had been marked by ruthless power grabs, regular abuses of constitutional propriety and naked appeals to popular anger. Many individuals, particularly among the propertied classes, found themselves squeezed with no way out. Chávez held elections and he won them, by hook or by crook. His country had oil, and he spent the proceeds. Venezuela became a more equal society and a more arbitrary state under his rule. He offered one sort of justice – the redistributive kind – at the expense of the other sort – the procedural kind. Democratic populism Chávez-style indicates that they don't go easily together.

Contemporary India suggests a similar lesson in reverse. Indian democracy has survived more or less intact since its birth in 1947 (minus a brief autocratic interlude under Indira Gandhi in the mid-1970s). Its constitution, inspired by Western models, was designed to protect the state from rampant populism. It is complex, intricate and rife with overlapping jurisdictions. Local politics competes with national politics, politicians with bureaucrats, populist democracy with the rule of law. The result has been a massive, clumsy, inefficient yet lasting politics of restraint. India continues to function as a constitutional democracy, which has brought many benefits (including the end of famine). But it has failed to solve the problem of inequality. India's recent economic growth has been very unevenly distributed. The middle class has rapidly expanded, and there has been a vast accumulation of wealth among the super-rich elite. Meanwhile the majority of Indians still live in poverty. Although almost no one starves to death, millions of Indian children continue to suffer from malnutrition and many of them die as a result. Indian democracy has not redressed the balance of structural injustice.

Amartya Sen, in conjunction with the American

philosopher Martha Nussbaum, argues that it does not have to be like this. Conventional liberal democracy on their account is a necessary but not a sufficient condition for political justice. You can't bypass it and expect the results to be anything but unjust in the long run. But nor can you rely on it. Instead, you have to expand it to include a wide range of political functions (or, as they call them, 'capabilities'), which include access to education, to healthcare and to equal opportunities for women, along with respect for emotional well-being. The negative politics of restraint needs to be extended until it becomes a positive politics of fulfilment. That's the aim. As Sen and Nussbaum are the first to admit, it hasn't happened yet.

How to turn a negative into a positive remains the unresolved moral challenge of modern politics. So far, the best answers – from neo-republicanism to Sen and Nussbaum's capabilities theory – remain answers on paper only. Recent history has not backed them up. We have had few practical lessons in how to do it in the period since Fukuyama proclaimed the end of history, which means that history is a long way from having come to an end. However, we have had one clear lesson in how not to do it. Among the negative achievements of democracy that I listed above is what has become known as 'democratic peace theory'. This is the idea that where you have widespread democracy you don't have war, because democracies won't fight each other. It is a view that can be traced back to the late eighteenth-century German philosopher Immanuel Kant, who argued that the path to 'perpetual peace' lay through the global expansion of republican politics: i.e., a politics of constitutional restraint. When citizens can restrain the bellicose instincts of their governments – above all, when the people who have to pay for wars through their taxes are in a position to prevent them – good sense will prevail. Kant was no blind optimist: he thought the path to peace would be a long and winding road. But it had to pass through what we now call democracy.

At the beginning of the twenty-first century some Western politicians, led by George W. Bush, wanted to find a short cut. If democracy equals the absence of war, then why not export democracy by force of arms in order to multiply its benefits? Wars to spread democracy could be viewed as an investment in the future peace of the world: abracadabra, a negative turned into a positive. In the aftermath of the attacks of 9/11, democratic peace theory got annexed to the war on terror, first in Afghanistan, then in Iraq. These wars had a dual purpose: to combat terrorism and to plant democracy in parts of the world where it was missing. Their aims were supposed to be mutually supportive. They turned out to be mutually destructive. The war on terror did not help to implant democracy, which is proving vulnerable in all those places to which it has been spread by force of arms since 2001. The attempt to implant democracy has not helped in the fight against terror, which has proliferated in many of the places where democracy has spread (above all, in Afghanistan and Iraq). To his credit, Fukuyama was one of those who warned what could go wrong. In 2003, before the invasion of Iraq, he broke with the boosters of democratic peace theory to argue that wars for peace are playing with fire. Politics is far too complex for such straightforward solutions. Fukuyama insisted that the institutional arrangements that constrain violence – from the rule of law to economic prosperity to democratic elections – are many and overlapping; they take time to work their magic together. Forcing it usually means wrecking it.

Democratic peace theory is a good example of the perilous gap that often separates knowing *that* in politics from knowing *how*. We know that democracies don't go to war together. But we don't know how to make it happen. We can't even be sure why it happens. Though Kant is often treated as a forerunner of contemporary liberal democracy, he is just as plausibly seen as a successor to Hobbes. In the field of international relations 'Hobbesian' is invariably translated as 'anarchic', since Hobbes said that states could do whatever they liked to defend themselves. It is assumed that means they will behave like individuals in the state of nature: by being fearful, mistrustful and trigger-happy. This is another misreading of Hobbes. The lawlessness of international politics does not have to result in a war of all against all. That's because there is a crucial difference between states and individuals: well-organised states are very hard to kill. You can't take them out when their backs are turned. Their backs are never turned: a state, unlike an individual, never switches off. States are not like people. They are like machines.

The vast, powerful, artificial entities created by modern politics have no real incentive to attack each other pre-emptively. The more powerful they are, the less incentive they have. The most powerful states of the modern age have been democracies (or 'republics', in Kant's terms), the United States being the most powerful of all. States like this have an excellent/terrifying record in war, depending on your point of view. They are hard to rouse but fearsomely difficult to defeat once roused and brutal in their willingness to deploy excessive force. Democracies may not fight each other, but they rarely lose the wars they do fight against non-democracies. (Their success rate in these contests is around 80 per cent.) So it is possible that one reason democracies don't fight each other is that they know better than to take on something so frightful. The democratic peace may not be proof of how nice democracies are. It may be evidence of how nasty they can be.

This is the most negative version of democratic peace theory. There are less negative versions, which suggest that liberal democracies encourage peace by facilitating free trade and the free movements of peoples among themselves. On this account, the European Union serves as an exemplification of what Kant had in mind. Yet even on this account, it is very hard to see how there could be any short cuts to peace, any more than there are currently short cuts to EU membership. (Turkey has been waiting for more than two decades now.) The problem remains that, outside of the magic circle of perpetual peace, its benefits are extremely unevenly distributed: democracies that exchange goods and people freely with each other can be very reluctant to extend those courtesies to anyone else. It is almost impossible to imagine the circumstances that would provoke the democracies of Western Europe to start fighting each other again. France is not going to resume its war with Germany any time soon. But it is not so hard to imagine the EU using force against some external enemy, if sufficiently alarmed and sufficiently confident of its ability to prevail. A future conflict with Africa – perhaps over mass migration – in which the Europeans deploy excessive force to get their way is still perfectly possible. What price perpetual peace then?

The truth is that we don't know how to fight wars for peace. We don't know how to turn democratic negatives into democratic positives. We don't know how to spread the benefits of politics to the people who need it most. We only know that we could do it better.

DROWNING CHILDREN

So far in this chapter I have been talking about the difficulties of doing good through politics. If it is so hard, why not bypass the politics altogether and simply focus on the need to do good? There are two reasons for thinking this might be the way to go. The first is practical: there are lots of ways to do good without relying on politics. We may not know how to export democracy, but plenty of other things are much easier to export. One is money: these days you just have to press a button and it zips wherever you want it to go. Food is another: people who are starving can be helped directly by being provided with the thing they immediately require. Many parts of the world, including Europe, have much more food than they know what to do with. Other parts have nowhere near enough. So move it!

The second reason to focus on the need to do good is that global inequality constitutes a moral failure as much as a political one. Allowing so many human beings to face a constrained and perilous existence when we have the resources to alleviate it can be viewed as a form of wickedness. That is how it has been painted by the moral philosopher Peter Singer, in a famous argument that draws an analogy with how we would behave if we encountered a drowning child. Imagine you pass a pond and you see a child about to go under. Would you dive in to help, if nothing was preventing you? Of course you would. No one would think twice, even if it were a serious inconvenience. Yes, your clothes will get wet, and yes, you might end up late for whatever you were on your way to do. So what? It would be unconscionable to walk on by. Now what if the child is thousands of miles away rather than right in front of your eyes, and starving or dying of a preventable disease rather than drowning? You still have the power to rescue the situation by extending your help: you can send money to stop it from happening. How can it be acceptable to walk on by in this case and not in the other? Why should mere physical distance make all the moral difference? Singer says that it can't. If you have the capacity to prevent a death and choose not to exercise it, your behaviour is morally indefensible, regardless of where the disaster is taking place. Pleading inconvenience – the money you spend to save a life is money you would rather have spent to make your own life a little more comfortable – is no excuse.

Singer argues that anyone in the West who has reached a comfortable level of affluence, beyond which any extra income is merely convenient rather than essential, has a moral obligation to give the surplus away to the planet's drowning children. What's the cut-off point? No one can say exactly, but another moral philosopher, Toby Ord, founder of the charity Giving What We Can, hit the news in 2009 by suggesting that an income of £30,000 a year was more than enough, and he would make do with £20,000. This made headlines because it is so rare to hear of people taking Singer's argument literally. Other moral philosophers have tried to pick holes in Singer's case, indicating that he has missed crucial features of our obligations to people with whom we have direct contact. Certainly the position Singer adopts is intensely morally demanding. But that's not the problem. Morality is meant to be demanding, otherwise what's the point of it? The real problem is politics. No matter how compelling Singer's argument is in moral terms, politics gets in the way.

Politics intrudes from two directions. First of all, it makes the inhabitants of stable, prosperous states – the ones with the power to help – insular and self-regarding. Inclusive political systems have unavoidably shrunken horizons because their attention is invariably directed inwards. There is persistent evidence that the inhabitants of modern democracies think that their governments are giving far more money away in foreign aid than they actually are. A 2013 poll in the United States revealed that Americans on average thought that overseas aid accounted for 25 per cent of the federal budget, when the true figure is around

1 per cent. Because of this misapprehension, nearly half of respondents listed cutting aid as their number one priority for reducing the budget deficit. Democratic politics doesn't necessarily make people selfish. But it does make them myopic. Citizens get used to referring their political choices to each other, not to anyone else. Moral philosophy might insist that physical distance does not matter. But inclusive politics reinforces the message that it does.

So the politics of successful states is one problem. The other is the politics of failed states. Telling individuals to bypass their governments and give money directly to the people who need it would be a more powerful message if potential donors could be sure their money would reach the people for whom it is intended. There is a big difference between rescuing a child with your bare hands and spending money to achieve the same result: in the second case you have to trust someone else to do it for you. Many of us do not have that trust. In the parts of the world where direct aid is most needed it is often impossible to ensure it gets through, because political instability and the threat of violence see much of it siphoned off by corrupt officials and predatory warlords. In the West, aid is associated with fuelling bad politics rather than bypassing it. Aid agencies do what they can to correct this impression, but it is an uphill struggle. The evidence is at best mixed. The moral clarity of the argument about rescuing drowning children is unavoidably diluted by the real-world messiness of providing practical help. Would we mind getting our clothes wet if what looked like a drowning child turned out to be a plastic bag someone has chucked away? We shouldn't, but we do.

Taken separately, these problems need not be an insu-
perable barrier to increasing transfers of resources from
the global rich to the global poor (and, as Ord points out,
an income of £30,000 puts anyone in the top 1 per cent of
global earners). If affluent citizens remained myopic but aid
always had glaringly beneficial results, the myopia would
probably ease over time as people were able to see the
good their generosity could do. If failed states remained an
obstruction but democratic citizens were more expansive
in their sympathies, then over time the consistent inflow
of resources would create the conditions to remedy state
failure. But, taken together, rich-world insularity and poor-
world instability are a deadly combination. The result is
that the crusade against global poverty increasingly tries
to bypass both, focusing instead on micro-initiatives and
technocratic fixes. Significant progress has been made with
these methods, and there is growing evidence that extreme
poverty is being reduced by the smart application of help
to the places where it can do most good. But technocratic
fixes do nothing to remedy the indifference of the global
rich to the plight of the global poor. If anything, they reinforce it. That's the trouble with technocracy: it indicates that
the problem is too complicated for us to solve. Someone else
needs to take care of it.

A similar difficulty applies to the extension of our help to
another group of people who might need it: the unborn. The
gloomiest prognostications for the likely effects of contin-
ued climate change is that there will eventually be a lot more
drowning children. As temperatures rise and sea levels rise
with them, huge numbers of people are going to be exposed

to catastrophic environmental hazards. The worst-affected areas will be among the poorest parts of the planet, in Asia and Africa. The rich countries of the North may end up better off. Global warming looks like a good deal for Canadians and a very bad one for the Congolese. Wealthy nations have the option to spend resources now to try to alleviate the coming threat: not vast outlays, but significant ones. (The Stern report indicates that 1–2 per cent of global GDP would be needed to make a difference.) But so far we have done next to nothing. Why? Because the people with the resources are not the ones who are most at risk. Because we don't believe that the money we allocate would be spent efficiently. And because people alive now don't seem unduly concerned about the plight of people not yet born. The time horizons of successful democracies tend to be as shrunken as their geographical ones.

There is a tempting analogy here with Singer's argument about drowning children. Would you save a child who was going to die in the next few minutes? Yes. Then presumably you feel the same about a child who would die in the next few days without your immediate intervention (perhaps a few more minutes in the water would result in lingering hypothermia). And if a few days doesn't make a difference, why should a few years? Indeed, why should the life of a child now be worth more than the life of a child at any point in the future, even if that child does not yet exist? One day, a hundred days, one year, a hundred years: it's all the same if you have the power to prevent the disaster. Distance in time is no more morally significant than distance in space. An avoidable death is still an avoidable death.

Yet the moral force of this argument quickly gets diluted by political realities. The uncertainties created by physical distance are exacerbated in the case of time. How can we be sure that future people really need our help, or that the help we provide will eventually reach them? Given the pace of technological change, fifty or a hundred years in the future can seem impossibly remote. Life will be so different then that our help may turn out to be wasted because we have targeted it at the wrong thing. Perhaps future generations will be better placed to deal with the problems of global warming than we are, in which case we should concentrate on safeguarding technological innovation instead of worrying about distributive justice between the living and the unborn. This argument gains force if you think about what might have happened if people a hundred years ago had decided to husband their resources so as to pass them on to us. We would now be worse off, because their selflessness would have stifled innovation and economic growth. Spending in the present is an investment in the future. Saving for the future can be a waste of present resources.

Environmental sceptics (or 'realists', as they like to call themselves) often point out that we've been here many times before. Modern history is full of panics about impending catastrophe: the food is running out! (the 1790s); the coal is running out! (1860s); the oil is running out! (1920s); the planet is getting colder! (1960s); the population is going to explode! (1970s); and so on. If each of these warnings had been taken literally at the time and everyone had pulled in their horns simultaneously, then the problem might never have got fixed, because what fixed it was innovation, not retrenchment. Yet there is a serious danger to this kind of techno-optimism. It is possible that some of our present actions may produce runaway future effects that cannot be controlled. Consumption in the present doesn't just make productive use of our current resources. It can also store up long-term harms that will be felt only by people not yet born. The time delay is what matters here. The assumption that technological advance will enable future generations to solve their problems when they need to depends on the problems revealing themselves in a timely manner. What if the damage only becomes visible when it is too late to do anything to prevent it? If people alive one hundred years ago had done something terrible to the environment whose effects were only being experienced now, we would still have the right to feel aggrieved. The fact that they also bequeathed us the internet would be little consolation.

One way to negotiate these problems is with the principle known as discounting, which says that, although we must consider the future impact of our actions, we can discount some of it because of uncertainty about what additional resources future generations will possess. If you spend a dollar today to help someone who in fifty years' time might be ten times richer than you, then it's the equivalent of spending 10 dollars on them. The discounting principle says that under those circumstances you only need to spend

10 cents to treat them fairly. Yet even a heavily discounted view of the future can be too much for modern democracies, where any long-term thinking tends to get drowned out by the short-term demands of the electoral cycle.

At present democratic politics in the West is heavily skewed in favour of the interests of the old over those of the young. Currently existing pensioners get far more attention than future pensioners; students get squeezed in favour of retirees; old-age benefits are often the last to go when cuts must be made. This is because old people vote more regularly than young people and democratic politicians are never far away from the next election. If the young people who could vote but don't barely get a look in, what hope for children and the unborn, who don't get to vote at all? Some political philosophers say the only solution is to enfranchise children of all ages and to give the unborn representatives who can speak for them in parliament. Debates could then include arguments that begin: 'On behalf of the seven-year olds who sent me here …' or 'Speaking as the MP for the year 2050 …'. But this is fantasy politics. Actually existing voters – including the old – are never going to allow it.

The direct transfer of resources from those who have them to those who really need them is a moral imperative and a practical nightmare. Politics keeps getting in the way.

A GOVERNMENT FOR THE WORLD

So here's a final solution: instead of trying to bypass politics, why don't we scale it up to match the size of the problem? Voters in rich states have got used to letting their governments take some of their income and having it redirected towards needier fellow citizens. Why not try it on an international level? Though inequality has been growing in the United States, it is nothing like the gulf that exists between the US and the poorest parts of Africa. If a world government could redistribute global resources on the same scale that the federal US government redistributes between, say, New York and Louisiana, the results would be transformative. (Poorer US states get significant transfers from wealthier parts of the Union, amounting to hundreds of billions of dollars a year.) All it takes is a central authority with the coercive power to levy taxes and then decide how they should get spent. No such authority presently exists at the global level. Perhaps it is time to make one.

The dream of a world state has been around for about as long as there have been nation-states competing and squabbling over the planet's resources. It can seem like a no-brainer: if states have the power to enforce agreement but can't agree among themselves, don't you need a super-state to enforce agreement between states? Kant considered this option when he discussed the idea of perpetual peace at the end of the eighteenth century. But he decided it would be a bad idea. The reason he gave was the obvious one. Such a super-state would be too big. A world government would be too cumbersome and too remote from the lives of the individuals who had to live under it. Kant thought that, whatever new connections are made by advances in global communications and the spread of international trade, there is still too much global diversity to be accommodated within a single political structure. A state large enough to find room for everyone on the planet would end up hopelessly distant from the actual political experiences of many of its citizens. That argument still looks compelling today. World government remains a bad idea. As always in politics, it's worth thinking about the worst that could happen. The worst that could happen with a global state would be a global civil war.

Sometimes it is assumed that Hobbes's view of politics points in the direction of a world state. If individuals in the state of nature can see that they need to stop fighting and hand over power to a higher authority, why don't sovereign states agree to the same thing? The answer, as I have already indicated, is that states are not like natural human beings. They are far harder to kill. Many states – and not just the most powerful ones – will choose to take their chances on violence. This means that it is very difficult to engineer the circumstances in which all states feel as afraid of each other as individuals feel in the state of nature. There would have to be some truly cataclysmic collective threat to get the United States, Russia and China to think they were all so vulnerable

that they had no option but to pool their separate right to defend themselves. Perhaps an asteroid on collision course with earth would do it, or an invasion from outer space. These are the scenarios that really excite Hollywood producers (which is why it's usually the US president who ends up taking charge). Until something like that actually happens, we are still in the realm of fantasy politics.

However, the practical difficulties in the way of creating a truly global politics have not stopped people from trying. Modern political history is punctuated by repeated attempts to establish an institutional framework for nation-states to come together to settle their differences. These enterprises usually gain momentum in the aftermath of disastrous international conflicts. The First World War spawned the League of Nations. The Second World War gave birth to its successor, the United Nations. These organisations fall some way short of what would be required for a world state: they possess parliaments but not an army, and they lack tax-raising powers. They have also done as much to reinforce

existing power differentials between states as to correct for them.

The League of Nations was the brainchild of British and American statesmen who wanted to cement their respective nations' grip on global politics. They never really agreed on how this could be done in a way that could satisfy both. (One reason members of the US Senate ultimately refused to sanction American participation in the League was that the end-product looked to some of them like an extension of the British Empire.) The constitution of the UN equally reflects the realities of post-war imperial power politics. The Security Council provides the big beasts of the international scene – the US, Russia and now China – with a veto over anything decided by the small fry. It also provides them with a veto to use against each other. This is enough to prevent the UN from morphing into a world government. It still seems likely that the only way for that to happen would be for one global empire to conquer the rest.

A world state is a pipe dream. But there are lots of international organisations that stand somewhere between the politics of individual nation-states and the ideal of a single government for everyone. The UN has multiple subsidiary agencies, in its various guises as peacekeeper, mediator, promoter of health and education and defender of human rights (you can find a list of them at http://www.un.org/en/aboutun/structure/). Then there are the continental unions, of which the EU is one. The African Union has grown in strength during the decade and a bit of its existence, reflecting the growing economic prosperity of some African states. There are trade zones such as NAFTA, sporting bodies like

FIFA, scientific organisations like the WHO. There is the World Bank and the International Criminal Court. There is the G8 and the G20. There are numerous charitable NGOs of wide international reach. The list could go on and on. Finally it would have to include the many multinational corporations that operate in almost every national jurisdiction in the world. Some of these perform roles and provide benefits that we might normally associate with government: education, training, welfare, security. If you get a job with Google, no matter where you are, you are going to be very well looked after. The distribution of these benefits is extremely patchy, and a lot depends on finding yourself in the right place at the right time. (It's incredibly hard to get a job with Google.) But in some places the same is true of government.

Nonetheless, despite this mind-boggling proliferation of international organisations, there are really just two basic models for international politics outside of a world state. One is the technocratic model. Here politics is understood as something that can be rationalised and improved by being parcelled out into narrow areas of technical expertise. The underlying idea is pragmatic: international co-operation functions best when it devolves onto specialists who know how to make things work. This model often relies on the ever-growing body of international law to regulate governments and to reconcile conflicts. It suffers from the failing of all technocratic models of politics: it is insufficiently political. It assumes that non-experts will put up with being told what to do by experts so long as the expertise continues to deliver benefits. That won't happen. First, people get tired of being told what to do by experts. They will eventually want more input themselves. Second, even experts can't keep delivering the benefits. Sooner or later they will screw up. When that happens, the international technocratic order won't be able to handle the fall out. Politics will erupt.

The alternative model sees international politics as an extension of the modern state rather than as a limitation on it. There are ways to scale up without going all the way to world government. Take the EU. At present it is sliding towards technocracy. Bankers and lawyers, regulators and bureaucrats all tiptoe around national politicians, trying to find a way to keep the benefits going without upsetting anyone too much. Any push towards a federal European state is very muted. Germans don't want to give their money to Greeks because they don't see them as fellow citizens. For now no one wants to force the issue. But a genuine European state, or its equivalent in other parts of the world – a West African state, a pan-Pacific state, a Central American state – is the only plausible rival to creeping technocracy. It would require a radical change of course. In the EU it would mean European-wide political parties, fielding candidates in European-wide elections, standing on European-wide platforms. Real politics, real choices, real conflicts, and at the end of it all someone with the power to pool the resources of an entire continent if

the situation demanded it. How big a change would this be? Imagine the British electorate, currently flirting with UKIP and tempted by a referendum that will offer the chance to leave the EU altogether, instead voting for a Polish or a Spanish or a Danish politician to be president of Europe and accepting the result as legitimate. Then the victorious politician using his or her legitimacy to levy taxes on British citizens at rates that served the wider interests of the European Union. And British citizens feeling that they had no choice but to pay. *That* big a change.

Scaling up would have to go along with some scaling down. Large political organisations, covering diverse populations and extensive territories, need to leave plenty of room for local politics. New technology could help to make a revival of local politics possible. To take one, seemingly banal example: the advent of 3-D printing could soon empower individuals and local communities to take charge for themselves of the physical production of the goods they need. It will become less and less necessary for vast quantities of these goods to be moved around the world. But this new localism will not work on its own. It will take political protection and political organisation to maintain it in the face of the forces of global capitalism, which will continue to sweep around the world, hoovering up money and resources. International politics needs to be big if it is to preserve the small. 3-D printers can't do the political work, any more than mobile phones can.

The problem with big-scale solutions is that they are too political. Someone would have to force the issue. Nation-states are not incentivised to pool their resources in this way.

The softly, softly technocratic approach is easier because so much can be done by stealth. Getting people – politicians as well as ordinary citizens – to sign up for a new kind of politics almost always takes a shock to the system. The traditional form this shock takes is war. The original EEC (the forerunner of the EU) was made possible only by the catastrophe of the Second World War and the looming disaster of the Cold War, which finally succeeded in banging French and German heads together. It is hard to see how a step-change to the next level of European federation – banging German and Greek heads together – will be possible in the absence of something similar. The US federal government is a product of two wars: the War of Independence from Britain, which produced a national government, and the Civil War, which finally gave that government the power to extend its coercive authority across the whole continent. Civil war looks very remote in Europe today because we are no longer interested in that sort of step-change. Reviving the prospect of war in order to achieve it seems a very high price to pay.

Peace promotes easy options. Easy options encourage bad politics. Bad politics threatens disaster. Disaster invites political salvation. It is a precarious business. Given time, and luck, we may get there without anything too terrible happening. The questions are: will we have the luck? And do we have the time?

EPILOGUE
CATASTROPHE

Societies that fail to adapt to the challenges they face eventually fall apart. The planet is littered with monuments to political systems that finally ran out of road, leaving only their relics behind. The Parthenon in Athens stands as a testament to the passing glory of ancient Athenian democracy, which flourished for two hundred years and then died at the hands of Philip of Macedon and his son Alexander the Great. The huge monolithic stone heads on Easter Island were produced by a flourishing island community as symbols of the power and purpose of its leading inhabitants; the competition to build bigger and better statues eventually used up the island's natural resources, resulting in starvation and ruin. Lenin's tomb in Moscow once stood as the focal point for global communism, honouring the man who had devised a politics that was going to conquer the future; now that the future is here, his mausoleum has become just another tourist trap. Are the liberal democracies that Fukuyama said were the end of history destined to go the same way? Will the Capitol in Washington sooner or later join the list of magnificent ruins?

There are two reasons to think that the fate of democracy may be different. The first is that the most successful states of the present have access to resources that no previous society could match. We are enormously richer,

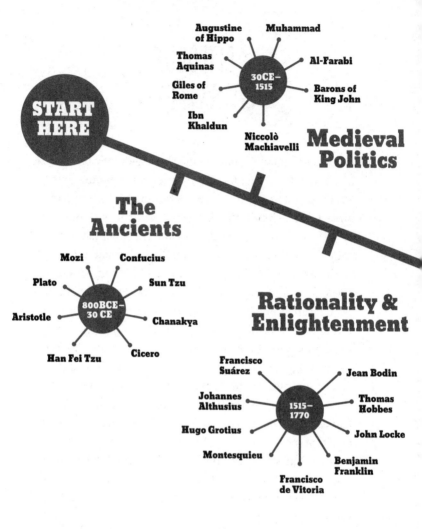

START HERE

30CE–1515
- Augustine of Hippo
- Muhammad
- Thomas Aquinas
- Al-Farabi
- Giles of Rome
- Barons of King John
- Ibn Khaldun
- Niccolò Machiavelli

Medieval Politics

The Ancients

800BCE–30 CE
- Mozi
- Confucius
- Plato
- Sun Tzu
- Aristotle
- Chanakya
- Han Fei Tzu
- Cicero

Rationality & Enlightenment

1515–1770
- Francisco Suárez
- Jean Bodin
- Johannes Althusius
- Thomas Hobbes
- Hugo Grotius
- John Locke
- Montesquieu
- Benjamin Franklin
- Francisco de Vitoria

POLITICS
Want to know more?

José Mariá
Luis Mora

James Madison

Immanuel Kant

Mary
Wollstonecraft

Edmund Burke

Georg Hegel

Thomas Paine

Carl von
Clausewitz

1770–
1848

Thomas Jefferson

John C.
Calhoun

Johan Gottfried
Herder

Jeremy Bentham

**Vive la
Revolution**

Auguste
Comte

Simón
Bolivar

**Mass
Politics**

Giuseppe Mazzini

John Stuart Mill

Abraham Lincoln

Pierre-Joseph
Proudhon

Mikhail Bakunin

Henry David
Thoreau

Alexander Herzen

Karl Marx

1848–
1910

Alexis de Tocqueville

Ito Hirobumi

Friedrich Nietzsche

George Sorel

Peter Kropotkin

José Marti

Emmeline Pankhurst

Jane Addams

Theodor Herzl

Sun Yat-Sen

Beatrice Webb

Max Weber

better-educated, better-informed, healthier and longer-lived than any human beings have ever been. We can draw on vast and sophisticated networks of communication. We keep inventing new stuff at a prodigious rate. The pace of change is only going to accelerate. It is hard to see how societies like these could get stuck for long.

The second reason is that modern democracy is inherently adaptable. Democracies are good at avoiding the worst political outcomes because democratic citizens are so irritable and impatient, constantly pushing for something a little better than what they have. When democracies make mistakes – which they frequently do – they don't plough on with them to the bitter end. They change course. The politics of restraint has proved good at correcting for the most serious errors of judgement that politicians can make. Bad leaders get kicked out of office; slightly less bad leaders replace them. Slowly, painfully, the system rights itself. Autocratic regimes, which are often better at taking snap decisions, are worse at spotting when those decisions are the wrong ones. Dictators and tyrants are the ones who lead their people over a cliff.

However, there are other reasons for thinking that these might be false consolations. The first is that the democracies are not masters of their own fate. Our world is now so interconnected that failure in one place can lead to a cascade of disastrous consequences for everyone. Contemporary Denmark is as comfortable a place to live as human beings have ever found. But Denmark would be powerless to protect itself from disastrous mismanagement somewhere else on the planet. Even the most powerful states are too dependent on each other to be confident that they can be immunised from each other's mistakes. The United States and China are competing experiments in forms of technocratic government. The democratic version, which combines elections with financial expertise – professional politicians with central bankers – is the more adaptable. The autocratic version, which combines one-party rule with managerial expertise – party cadres with engineers – is the more decisive. The problem with the adaptable system is that it can be indecisive. The problem with the decisive system is that it can struggle to adapt. When either of these experiments goes wrong, the knock-on effects will be felt everywhere. Another financial crash in the US or a political revolution in China would have consequences that are very hard to predict. In the worst-case scenario, the two systems could still find themselves at war. If that happens, all bets are off. Even in Denmark.

The second reason to be worried is that history may not be a reliable guide. The challenges that states face in the twenty-first century are different from those they have faced in the past. The difference is in the time-scale. The advantage of democratic adaptability depends on there being time to adapt. That may not be the case for the most serious threats the democracies are likely to face. In some respects time is too short. One of the striking features of the financial crash of 2008 was just how quickly politicians had to act to stave off disaster. They got through that one by the skin of their teeth, but there is no guarantee that next time they will be so lucky. Meanwhile, the consequences of the crash will be playing out for a generation or more. Recovery has been slower than for any previous recession, slower even than the Great Depression in the early 1930s. A large cohort of young people across the Western world is out of employment, with no prospect of finding a job any time soon. Austerity and the paying down of public and private debt are liable to continue for the foreseeable future. Voters are told that in the long run they will benefit. Yet democracy still works to the timetable of the electoral cycle, with its premium on regular, incremental improvements in people's standard of living. The time-scales are out of joint. Politicians have a few hours to save the world; voters have to wait decades to see the benefits. It is not clear how democracy will adapt to this challenge.

The most acute version of the conundrum relates to climate change and the threat of environmental catastrophe. The long lag before the effects of climate change will be felt make it very difficult for elected politicians to take pre-emptive action, conscious as they are that the people who pay the price won't be the people who see the benefits. Yet if we never take pre-emptive action, and if the gloomier scenarios predicted by the current science turn out to be correct, then the consequences are likely to catch us unawares. At some point, the long-term threat of environmental degradation will reveal itself as an immediate disaster: a massive flood, a calamitous harvest failure, the mass movement of peoples, another war. At that point democratic adaptability will kick in. But by then it may be too late. Autocratic regimes like China might be able to take more decisive action in the present to deal with the long-term effects of climate change. China's rulers do not have to worry about getting re-elected.

So if China's technocrats decide to green a Chinese city, they can, within practical limits, make it happen. However, Chinese technocracy won't resolve climate change on its own. And when the consequences of democratic inaction reveal themselves in the future, the Chinese political system may be insufficiently adaptable to cope.

The final problem is that democratic adaptability can morph into democratic complacency. We have reached the point where there is good historical evidence that democracies eventually rise to meet the challenges they face. The transition from Hobbes's world to our world is a story of the successful adaptation by inclusive states to whatever history could throw at them. Democracy survived the Great Depression. It saw off fascism. It outlasted communism. It eventually enfranchised almost all its citizens. Violence fell away. Prosperity spread. Democracies have not always responded to threats and injustices in a timely fashion, but they have got there in the end. It is tempting to assume that this process can continue indefinitely. We will get our act together when we need to.

In late October 2013, the US Congress shut down the Federal government as part of an intractable and poisonously partisan dispute over the funding of President Obama's healthcare reforms. It looked like a recklessly cavalier act: politicians choosing to pull the plug on government because they can't agree on an important piece of legislation. The causes of the growing partisanship and rancour in American politics are many. But one of them must be this: politicians behave so cavalierly because they think the system can survive it. They don't believe that they have really pulled the plug on government. American democracy has got through much worse in the past and survived. So it's assumed it can survive this. When the dust settles, the system will adapt. And perhaps it will. But this is brinkmanship that imagines the real brink is always some way off. You can flirt with disaster because it is only flirting. No American politician wants to renege on America's debt or stop paying the bills. They threaten to do it only because they believe it will never happen.

This is politics as a game of chicken. Games of chicken are harmless, until they go wrong, at which point they become fatal. Flirting with disaster at a time of rapid change and increasing global interconnectivity risks meeting with disaster just when you least expect it. The US government may believe it will always honour its debts in the end. But its creditors, which include the Chinese government, may get tired of all the games. China's technocrats could choose to pull the plug themselves by looking for somewhere else to park their cash. Then the US is in real trouble. Cavalier democratic politicians can easily lose control of events. Relying on adaptability to save them only makes it more likely that they will eventually hit the rocks.

None of this means democracy is doomed. Nothing in politics is pre-ordained. There are still plenty of grounds for optimism in a world that is better off than it has ever been, in which poverty as well as violence is on the retreat and where technology promises limitless new opportunities. The threat of catastrophe remains real, however. Things could still go terribly wrong. Relying on technology to save us will not be enough. We need to recognise the risks posed by global interconnectivity, by the time-lags between our present actions and their long-term consequences, and by our growing complacency about what politics can achieve. The only way to meet the challenges of the future is to make the best use we can of the representative institutions of the modern state. Given the size of those challenges, the institutions of the state will almost certainly have to be scaled up to match them as well as being scaled down to prevent them from becoming too remote. This will involve difficult choices and dangerous moments. Nothing about it will be easy. But it can't be done by stealth or by crossing our fingers. It can only be done through politics.

Politics still matters.

REFERENCES

In chronological order (not the order they appear in the book), these are the writings and authors that are referred to in the text:

- Thomas Hobbes, *Leviathan* (1651), ed. Richard Tuck (Cambridge: Cambridge University Press, 1996)
- Charles-Louis de Montesquieu, *The Spirit of the Laws* (1748), ed. H. Stone (Cambridge: Cambridge: Cambridge University Press, 1991)
- Immanuel Kant, 'Perpetual peace: a philosophical sketch' (1795), in *Political Writings*, ed. H. L. Reiss (Cambridge: Cambridge University Press, 1991)
- Benjamin Constant, 'The liberty of the ancients compared to the liberty of the moderns' (1819), in *Political Writings*, ed. Biancamaria Fontana (Cambridge: Cambridge University Press, 1988)
- Max Weber, 'Politics as a vocation' (1919), in *Political Writings*, ed. P. Lassmann and R. Speirs (Cambridge: Cambridge University Press, 1994)
- James Burnham, T*he Managerial Revolution* (Westport, CT: Greenwood Press, 1941)
- George Orwell, *1984* (1948) (Harmondsworth: Penguin Classics, 2013)
- John Rawls, *A Theory of Justice* (Cambridge, MA: Harvard University Press, 1971)
- Francis Fukuyama, 'The end of history', *The National Interest,* 16 (1989), pp. 3–18.
- Peter Singer, 'The drowning child and the expanding circle', *New Internationalist* (April 1997)
- Cormac McCarthy, *The Road* (New York: Alfred Knopf, 2006)
- Christian Jungersen, *The Exception* (London: Orion, 2007)
- Nicholas Stern, *The Economics of Climate Change: The Stern Review* (Cambridge: Cambridge University Press, 2007)
- Martha Nussbaum, *Creating Capabilities: The Human Development Approach* (Cambridge, MA: Harvard University Press, 2011)
- Daron Acemoglu and James Robinson, *Why Nations Fail: The Origins of Power, Prosperity and Poverty* (London: Profile, 2012)

FURTHER READING

Introduction
- On what turned Denmark into Denmark, and what that says about the historical evolution of ordered political societies: Francis Fukuyama, *The Origins of Political Order* (London: Profile, 2012)

Chapter 1: Violence
- On the decline of violence over the long sweep of modern history (and much more markedly in recent times): Steven Pinker, *The Better Angels of Our Nature: A History of Violence and Humanity* (Harmondsworth: Penguin, 2012)
- For a lecture that explains what is so original about Hobbes's theory of the state, watch Quentin Skinner's 'What is the state? The question that will not go away', http://vimeo.com/14979551
- The best book about the idea of representation and its role in modern politics is still: Hanna Pitkin, *The Concept of Representation* (Berkeley, CA: University of California Press, 1967)
- A classic treatment of the problem of 'dirty hands', written at the time of the Vietnam War and provoked by some of its horrors: Michael Walzer, 'Political action: the problem of dirty hands', *Philosophy and Public Affairs*, 2 (1973), pp. 160–80
- A concise and lucid account of the rationale behind drone warfare and what's wrong with it: Stephen Holmes, 'What's in it for Obama? The drone presidency', *London Review of Books* (18 July 2013), pp. 15–18. http://www.lrb.co.uk/v35/n14/stephen-holmes/whats-in-it-for-obama

Chapter 2: Technology
- The best recent account of the relationship between government spending and technological revolution is: William H. Janeway, *Doing Capitalism in the Innovation Economy* (Cambridge: Cambridge University Press, 2012)
- On the close link between the rise of the new technology and the decay of American politics: George Packer, *The Unwinding: An Inner History of the New America* (London: Faber and Faber, 2013)
- An angry account of the narrowing of the political class in twenty-first-century Britain, written by a political insider: Ferdinand Mount, *The New Few, or A Very British Oligarchy* (London: Simon and Schuster, 2012).

- On the role of protectionism in stabilising developing countries: Ha-Joon Chang, *23 Things They Don't Tell You about Capitalism* (Harmondsworth: Penguin, 2011). Economists don't like this book, but it isn't really a book about economics. It's about politics.
- For a radical critique of the political implications of the latest developments in information technology: Evgeny Morozov, 'Information consumerism: the price of hypocrisy', *Frankfurter Allgemeine* (24 July 2013) http://www.faz.net/aktuell/feuilleton/debatten/ueberwachung/information-consumerism-the-price-of-hypocrisy-12292374.html

Chapter 3: Justice
- On the potentially fatal relationship between Rawlsian philosophy and fantasy politics: Raymond Geuss, *Philosophy and Real Politics* (Princeton, NJ: Princeton University Press, 2008)
- For Sen's most recent discussion of the idea of justice, which contains a critique of both Hobbes and Rawls, as well as a defence of the capabilities approach: Amartya Sen, *The Idea of Justice* (Cambridge, MA: Harvard University Press, 2009)
- An impassioned and almost persuasive account of why nothing is ever as bad as it seems: Matt Ridley, *The Rational Optimist: How Prosperity Evolves* (London: Fourth Estate, 2010)
- In this book I have said little about classical political philosophy. For a take on what the ancient Greeks might be able to tell us about ecology and justice: Melissa Lane, *Eco-Republic. What the Ancients Can Teach Us about Ethics, Virtue and Sustainable Living* (Princeton, NJ: Princeton University Press, 2011)
- An excellent history of attempts to find a truly global politics over the last two hundred years, including the chequered history of ideas of a world state: Mark Mazower, *Governing the World* (London: Allen Lane, 2012)

Conclusion
- For the long version of what I think is the relationship between democracy and catastrophe, past, present and future: David Runciman, *The Confidence Trap: A History of Democracy in Crisis from the First World War to the Present* (Princeton, NJ: Princeton University Press, 2013)

IDEAS IN PROFILE

SMALL INTRODUCTIONS TO BIG TOPICS

Ideas in Profile is a landmark series that offers concise and entertaining introductions to topics that matter.

ALREADY PUBLISHED

Politics
by David Runciman

Art in History
by Martin Kemp

Shakespeare
by Paul Edmondson

The Ancient World
by Jerry Toner

FORTHCOMING

Geography
by Carl Lee and
Danny Dorling

Criticism
by Catherine Belsey

Music
by Andrew Gant

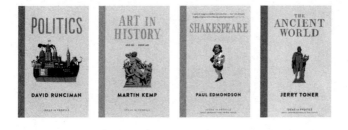